Fear of success—however we define that—can hold us back as much as fear of failure. In this book, Jeremy explores both of these psychological barriers, and in a humble and inspiring way, takes the reader step by step through a program for overcoming these barriers and moving towards achievement.

—Bruce Dines, VP Ventures at Liberty Global, Integrate Board Member

Jeremy's super smart and he gets the big picture. He realized that after sports he would need to do something more. He surrounded himself with very strong, very bright individuals who shared their insights, advice, and best practices. Now you too can learn those attributes in this book.

—Apolo Ohno, eight-time Olympic Medalist in Speed Skating

Sheer persistence and an unwavering positive attitude define Jeremy. Many know of his achievements in business and athletics, but few realize that he applies the same spirit and discipline to his philanthropic endeavors. He is a genuinely good person—one who you cannot help but root for and want to follow.

—Sam Landman, Managing Director at Comcast Ventures, Integrate Board Member

Throughout my life, I have come across incredible leaders, but Jeremy's ability to accomplish so many different feats consistently astounds me. As a friend and board member of Integrate, I am continually impressed by the way that he adapts and succeeds in any situation, even when it seems unachievable. This book helps to unlock your full potential by providing a roadmap on how to use adversity to strengthen your chances of ultimate success.

—Reggie Bradford, 3peat Entrepreneur and SVP at Oracle, Integrate Board Member

Part of what has made Jeremy's life so remarkable is that he takes on challenges and doesn't look back. When something doesn't work out he learns why and uses that knowledge to better himself. His book is the proverbial kick in the ass that most of us need when we start retreating or giving up on a challenge or a goal.

—Brad Feld, Entrepreneur, Author, Blogger, and Venture Capitalist at Foundry Group

Jeremy has emerged stronger from failures in his life and is truly the embodiment of positive energy in everything he does. In these pages Jeremy will show you how to move forward in business and in life without letting the disappointments get in your way.

—David Karnstedt, former Adobe Systems, Inc. SVP of Media and Advertising Solutions

Jeremy believes in possibility rather than limits. What stops most of us is our fear of failure, not failure itself. The dread of losing keeps us from the bold pursuits that create success. Jeremy, on the other hand, gets excited about an idea and pursues it with a fearless passion. What could you do if you didn't limit yourself from the start? Jeremy Bloom shows us how to focus on what's possible and just go for it!

—Jillaina Wachendorf, Wish of a Lifetime CEO

If you're in need of inspiration and actions to get you through the inevitable failures in business, and life, this book hits the mark. Jeremy recounts his journey from athletics to entrepreneurship with humility, sharing the backstory behind his very public defeats, and more importantly, revealing priceless lessons in competing for success. If you compete at anything—sports, business, or life—you need this book.

—Scott Blackmun, United States Olympic Committee CEO

I took Jeremy snowboarding for the first time. He went from being terrible at it to excelling in a matter of hours. Part of it was natural talent, but part was that he didn't fear failing. The rest was sheer tenacity. That embodies how Jeremy goes about learning new things and this book reflects it. He's done the research—practical and theoretical—and delivers great guidance on staying the course to reach success.

—Bill Maris, President and Managing Partner at Google Ventures

Jeremy has packed a lifetime of experience into 32 years. While he's led an extraordinary life thus far, the ups and downs he's experienced are something we can all connect with and learn from. His story is inspiring and the lessons he imparts are invigorating.

—Tony Bates, President of GoPro, Former CEO of Skype, Former VP of Cisco and Microsoft

Jeremy is proof that mindset is everything. He brings together the best people and supercharges them with his unique energy and inspiration. His Olympian work ethic and discipline works in the boardroom as well as it did on the ski slopes and football field. He will inspire you, too.

—Bing Gordon, General Partner at Kleiner Perkins and Former Chief Product Officer at Electronic Arts

Jeremy is one of the most compelling entrepreneurs I've ever worked with—actually, one of the most compelling individuals I've ever worked with. Always striving for the next goal, taking each setback as an opportunity to learn, surrounding himself with people he can learn from. Jeremy's never-give-up attitude is infectious and makes him extremely effective.

—Seth Levine, Managing Director at Foundry Group

FUELED
——— BY ———
FAILURE

USING DETOURS AND DEFEATS
TO POWER PROGRESS

JEREMY BLOOM

OLYMPIC SKIER • NFL PLAYER • CEO • PHILANTHROPIST

EP
Entrepreneur
PRESS®

Publisher: Entrepreneur Press
Cover Design: Andrew Welyczko
Production and Composition: Eliot House Productions

This publication is designed to provide accurate and authoritative information
in regard to the subject matter covered. It is sold with the understanding that
the publisher is not engaged in rendering legal, accounting or other professional services. If legal advice or other expert assistance is required, the services
of a competent professional person should be sought.

Library of Congress Cataloging-in-Publication Data
   Bloom, Jeremy, 1982-
     Fueled by failure: using detours and defeats to power progress/Jeremy Bloom.
       pages cm
      ISBN-13: 978-1-59918-563-7 (hardback)
      ISBN-10: 1-59918-563-6 (hardback)
       1. Success in business. 2. Failure (Psychology) 3. New business enterprises—
Management. 4. Organizational behavior. I. Title.
      HF5386.B556 2015
      658.4'09—dc23   2015000164

CONTENTS

ACKNOWLEDGMENTS XI

INTRODUCTION
GETTING FUELED XIII
    Baby Steps xiv

CHAPTER ONE
22 SECONDS TO GLORY 1
    One Move, One Moment 2
    My Other Dream 4
    The Road to the NFL—and Beyond 10

CHAPTER TWO
MOVING FORWARD: THE 48-HOUR RULE 13
    The Power of Deadlines 14
    48 Hours—and That's It 15
    How Much Time Do You Need? 16
    Three Mental Keys 17
    Passion, Resiliency, and Steve Jobs 21

Planting Seeds 22

Eliminating Distractions. 23

CHAPTER THREE

DEFINING FAILURE 25

What Is Failure? 26

The Weight of Failure 28

Embracing Failure to Succeed in Business. 30

CHAPTER FOUR

FORGET WINNING: REPROGRAM YOUR EGO 35

When Your Ego Gets in Your Way 36

Letting Go of the Need to Win 38

Workplace Motivators 44

CHAPTER FIVE

YOUR PERSONAL ROAD MAP FOR SUCCESS. 47

Plotting and Planning: Building in Increments 49

The Time Is Now. 51

In Search of Your Passion. 53

Making Pivots 60

My Personal Road Map 63

CHAPTER SIX

REDEFINE YOURSELF: YOUR NEW DESTINY 67

A New Challenge. 68

Taking Something with You 71

Keys to Changing Careers. 71

Successful Transitions. 73

CHAPTER SEVEN

MANAGEMENT, TEAM BUILDING, AND VICTIMS 79

Managing Your Team: Top-Down or Bottom-Up? 80

The Keys to Building a Strong Team. 81

Leaders vs. Victims 86

Anyone Can Stop Being a Victim 88

CHAPTER EIGHT

LOCKING ARMS: BUILDING A UNIFIED CULTURE 91

Creating a Culture That Works. 94
Cultural Cornerstones. 95
Optimism Delusion 102
Hiring to Match Your Culture. 104

CHAPTER NINE

THE ROLLER-COASTER RIDE 107

Taking a Ride 108
Managing Risk. 111
Tuning Out the Noise 111
Finding a Balance 113
In the End, It's All Worthwhile 114

CHAPTER TEN

MAKE A DIFFERENCE: DEFINING YOUR LEGACY 117

Looking Outside Yourself. 118
My Inspiration for Helping Seniors. 121
Starting a Nonprofit 122
Your Own Legacy 127

EPILOGUE

WHAT DOES IT ALL MEAN? 133

ABOUT THE AUTHOR 135

INDEX. 137

ACKNOWLEDGMENTS

Thank you first and foremost to my mom, Char, and dad, Larry. My parents have supported every dream that I have ever had in my life. They are my heroes and the two people that I look up to the most. I also want to thank my brother, Jordan, and my sister, Molly. As the youngest of three, I spent most of my childhood losing to both of them in just about everything. Those losses inspired me to set goals to become the best in the world. And to my dear grandmother Donna, who, at 89 years old, lives high in the Rocky Mountains in Keystone, Colorado, and volunteers every week at the elementary school and senior center.

I'd like to also thank the following people for contributing to this book: Tony Bates (former CEO of Skype and current president of GoPro), an entrepreneur who understands how to set an intention and accomplish his goals regardless of the circumstances; Brad Feld (managing director at Foundry Group), for his infinite wisdom and honesty, and for believing in me as an unproven entrepreneur; David Karnstedt (former CEO of Efficient Frontier), for being one of my closest business advisors; Bill Maris (managing director at Google Ventures), for first introducing me to the tech world and later becoming on of my closest friends; Eric Roza (CEO at Datalogix), for showing me that turning around a company when it seems impossible is, in fact, possible; Apolo Ohno (Olympic champion), for showing what hard work was all about as a young aspiring athlete; Karen Cogan (U.S. Ski Team sports psychologist), for helping me sharpen my ability to handle pressure; Jillaina Wachendorf (CEO at Wish of a Lifetime), for her infinite energy and passion in helping make sure the wishes of the oldest among us are fulfilled and don't die with them; and to Greg Besner, Dr. Sydney Finkelstein, Gail Sagel, Roger Staubach, and Brian Swette, all of whom I have not had the privilege of meeting personally, but whose stories inspire me. I would also like to thank Reggie Bradford, Seth Levine, Bruce Dines and Sam Landman for not only investing in me but for also becoming close friends and mentors along the way. I would not be where I am today if not for their support.

I would like to thank Sara Terry and the Brookdale Senior Living Team for believing in a vision for a national partnership with Wish of a Lifetime that has enriched the lives of senior citizens all across the country.

And thank you to Jillian McTigue, Rich Mintzer, Jennifer Merritt, and Karen Billipp for their work on this book for Entrepreneur Press.

GETTING FUELED

When I first started thinking about writing this book, I asked ten people what they thought about the title *Fueled by Failure*. All ten people told me not to use the word *failure* in the title. They said that the word brought such a negative connotation it would scare people away from reading the book. But every human will fail many times during his or her life, so why not be more prepared for it? The consistent negative bias toward the word failure only increased my desire to write this book.

The following pages are not simply about failure; they are actually much more about how to succeed against all odds. However, it is my strong belief that before you can become the world's best at anything you have to become great at leveraging adversity to refine your road map to greatness.

The most successful and happy people that I have been around in my life are those who are exceptional at doing this. They have developed the mental skills necessary to effectively deal with life's biggest curve balls, so they won't be thrown off their game. Throughout this book I will share stories of experiences and lessons I have picked up along the way that have helped me become more successful in athletics and startup life.

Baby Steps

We are born into this world and spend our first several years failing at everything. We fall down hundreds of times before we learn how to walk properly and we mix up the sounds of just about every word en route to learning proper English. We are thirsty for knowledge, and trial and error is our only method of learning. During these young years we haven't developed an ego yet, so the effect that failure has on us is almost nonexistent. We just keep trying and trying until we get it right. However, as we get older, we become more sensitive, our ego builds, and failure can have a much bigger effect on our determination to persevere and learn.

I once read that Thomas Edison failed nearly 10,000 times before inventing the electric light bulb. Edison claimed, in a now famous quote, "I have not failed 10,000 times—I've successfully found 10,000 ways that will not work."

For me, as a young athlete, I saw great athletes who were crushed by adversity, and later witnessed entrepreneurs struggle with failed businesses before they finally made their marks. I determined that whatever happened to me in my life, I would never allow myself to be defeated by failure. And although I have not yet mastered many of the skills discussed in this book, I am a passionate student of the topic.

Today, as I enjoy my position as CEO of Integrate, a venture-backed technology company that I cofounded a few years ago, I still look over my shoulder every day, aware that things could come crashing down around me at any moment. But I also recognize that my own path to success has always been paved with wins and losses, ups and downs, and both great and challenging times.

I wrote this book to share the trials and tribulations I went through to become the best skier in the world and an all-American football player, as well as my transition from professional sports to a startup founder entering a new and unknown world. I tell my story, from my early successes to falling on my face, to rebounding and fighting to pick myself back up. There is a chapter on reprogramming your ego, something paramount for me to become a world champion. I also explore the differences between being extrinsically motivated by others and intrinsically motivating yourself, a concept that I believe is crucial to master a happy and fulfilled life. And I share how I chart my road map for success.

I have had the great fortune of being surrounded by some of the best athletes and entrepreneurs in the world, and I have learned more from being around them than anything else in my life. Many of them share their wisdom and experience throughout this book. We'll look at changing careers and starting a business, along with management, team building, weeding out the victims, constructing a bad-ass culture, and how to manage the daily roller coaster of life.

The book concludes with an important chapter on leaving a legacy, which for me comes from starting a nonprofit that helps the oldest people in our country realize their dreams. It's my reminder that neither gold medals nor dollar bills define the most important things in life.

My goal is that by the end of this book you will become better equipped to use adversity to help you succeed while picking up some new ideas on how to make you, your team, or your business more successful.

CHAPTER ONE

22 SECONDS TO GLORY

I had 22 seconds to make a 23-year-old dream come true.

As I stood in the staging area at the 2006 Winter Olympics, in Torino, Italy, I thought about how I wanted to be able to call myself an Olympic champion. I thought about all my friends around the world watching me on TV and about my dad back home in Colorado and my mom who was in the grandstands waiting for me below. I flashed back to the years I spent competing in regional competitions around Colorado, the phone call I received at 15 when I found out that I had made the U.S. National Team, and the thousands of hours that I had spent preparing myself for this moment.

Images shot through my mind of the journey that had brought me to this point. I remembered the time, at 10 years old, when I first watched mogul skiing in the Olympics with my dad and my mom. My dad has a passion for the Olympics that goes back to the Carl Lewis days at the 1984 games and continues to this day. When a U.S. athlete stands atop the podium and "The Star-Spangled Banner" plays, he gets very emotional. My dad was my first football coach and ski coach, and my hero. I wanted nothing more in my life than to win an Olympic gold medal, not only for myself but also for my family. The thought of my family watching me as I stood on top of that Olympic podium, with a gold medal wrapped around my neck, was a major driving force in my lifelong quest.

I had won more consecutive World Cup races than any freestyle skier in history the year before—I was skiing great in 2006, and this was my moment. I had trained well all week and knew that I was going to ski flawlessly.

One Move, One Moment

As I slid into the starting gate, I got my first glimpse of the 230-meter mogul course where my fate would be decided. It was a beautiful night in Torino; the snow sparkled off the bright lights like a Manhattan sidewalk on a warm summer evening. I went over the three key things I needed to remember:

1. *Mind like a river.* Any thought that might come up that didn't have to do with my run would flow from the front of my head out the back. Nothing can stay still in a fast-moving river. This was also how I moved quickly past any self-defeating thoughts like "I'm going to fall," "I'm going to miss my top jump," or "I don't feel ready."
2. *Live downstairs.* I imagined myself downstairs in a cellar where no thoughts from the outside could get in. This was my way of eliminating any thought that wasn't focused on the skiing task at hand. It helped me achieve tunnel vision.
3. *Focus on your skills.* They are what will get you down this mountain every time. This was my method of going back to the basics.

I had an unusual sense of confidence that day. In my head I knew I was going to ski up to my potential. Finally, the judges were ready; my time had come. I wasn't nervous. My moment was now!

"Three, two, one," over the loudspeaker, and I pushed out of the gate. I felt the snow under my skis and quickly got into the top jump. I nailed my takeoff and landed my 720 iron-cross perfectly. As I landed, I started to accelerate faster and faster. The snow was icier than it had been in training. I felt myself getting a bit out of control, but I was determined to fight my skis back underneath me. I got it back together quickly and was flying into the bottom air. The takeoff on my D-spin 720 was not perfect, and I landed with a small compression. But I blazed through the bottom section of the course to the finish line. My heart immediately dropped—I knew it wasn't my best run.

Even though I wanted to win a medal, in reality, my biggest goal at the Olympics was to ski to my potential. If I did that, everything else would take care of itself. But I had made one mistake, and I knew it would cost me. The only question was how much. In those fleeting moments while I awaited my score, I felt the same gut-wrenching feeling I had experienced when I was 19 years old and participating in the 2002 Salt Lake City Olympics. That year, I had been the number-one ranked skier in the world, but I made a small mistake on my final run and it cost me an opportunity to medal.

My score came up. I was in fourth place with two skiers to go. My dreams of becoming an Olympic champion were over. I had prepared my entire life for this one moment and I knew there would not be another opportunity. Skiing through the media gauntlet that awaited me, I tried to smile, said the right things, and kept myself together, masking the disappointment as best I could. My mom came over, hugged me, and told me she was very proud of me. My mom was my biggest supporter and fan. She flew all over the world to see me compete and had not missed a single football game I played in during high school and college. Yet she always cared more about how I treated other people and how I handled winning and losing than she did about where I placed or whether I won.

When I returned to my apartment in Torino, I closed the door, sat down on the bed, and, well, that was it. I lost it. Tears flowed down my face. A torrent of emotion flooded over me. I wanted to crawl outside of my body because the pain was so unbearable. It was the lowest moment of my athletic life; I felt totally defeated once again on skiing's biggest stage.

I woke up the next morning hoping that it was all just a bad dream. Still engulfed in the emotion of what had occurred, I kept replaying the run again and again in my mind. I didn't want to talk to anyone, I just wanted to keep to myself and be alone. But there wasn't much time for mourning and self-pity. Within 48 hours' time, I had to move on. There was another dream that wasn't going to wait for me to recover from this devastating emotional blow: football.

My Other Dream

The next day, I boarded a plane to Indianapolis for the 2006 NFL Combine, the showcase for college football players to perform physical and mental tests in front of National Football League scouts, coaches, and general managers. It was the prelude to being drafted by an NFL team. In spite of the failure on the slopes, I needed to focus all my attention on football. At the time, becoming a professional football player was my other dream.

This would be one of the first times I truly felt what it meant to be fueled by your own failure, to take the negative feelings from the stumbles and rather than let them take control of you, instead use the power of failure to boost what came next. (I'll talk more about what failure looks like and how to take control of it in Chapter 3.)

I couldn't let the pain I felt about the end of my Olympic dream cloud my mind—or my chances of making an NFL team. I would come back to this idea of letting things go over and over in my athletic career and my entrepreneurial life.

My love of football came from my dad's love for the Denver Broncos and our hero, John Elway. He was drafted in 1983 by the Denver Broncos, a year after I was born. Growing up, I was a huge Elway fan. He was the ultimate competitor. He let his playing do the talking, treated people well, and was a humble leader. His goal was to take the Broncos to a Super Bowl title, and he accomplished that twice. I wanted to be a part of that same football ethos.

My Double Life: Downhill and Downfield

At the age of eight, I began competing locally in ski competitions and won in my age group for six years straight. In skiing I often heard people say that I was a prodigy from a young age, while in football at every level I heard that I was too small to play.

By the time I was ten years old, my dad reached the limit of his coaching abilities and signed me up for a ski team in Breckenridge, Colorado. Two of the greatest mogul coaches in history were associated with that team, Scott Rawles—who later became my Olympic team coach for many years—and John Dowling, who had been an Olympic coach and is the freestyle program director at the Ski & Snowboard Club Vail.

Not long after becoming part of Team Breckenridge, I also started playing Pop Warner football en route to making my junior high school team. Then, at 15, I became the youngest person at that time to make the U.S. Mogul Freestyle Ski Team. My ski coaches wanted me to quit playing football and move to a ski academy in the mountains. But I had always been a weekend skier, playing football during the week, and going to public schools in Loveland, Colorado, like a regular kid. I didn't want to give up that much of my life, especially not football, where I made my high school team. So I opted to stay put and maintain a somewhat normal life, getting the public school experience, enjoying homecoming, prom, and all sorts of teen activities—things that I wouldn't trade for anything.

In my freshman year of high school I played quarterback and defensive back. My sophomore year, at the urging of my coach, Tony Davis, who was a prolific running back at Nebraska, I switched to wide receiver, and this move allowed me to start on the varsity team. Midway through my senior year of high school, the University of Colorado offered me a full scholarship to play football.

Meanwhile, as part of the U.S. Ski Team, I was now competing and winning in freestyle events on the Nor-Am tour run by the International

Ski Federation. At the age of 17, I also won big series skiing events in the Pro-Am series and had become the best skier that was not yet competing at the World Cup level. It seemed obvious that I would be chosen to compete in a full World Cup season. But I was not selected. I was confused and frustrated. Without World Cup starts it was nearly impossible for me to make the Olympic team the next year, so I quit skiing in 2001 to focus on football. I lived on campus at the University of Colorado and trained with the team. Our strength and conditioning coach was the world famous Doc Kries. Kries kicked our asses every day—there just isn't any other way to put it. I didn't miss a single day of off-season conditioning and completely reshaped my concept of what hard work meant.

But then, that July I got a call from my skiing agent Andy Carroll. The U.S. Ski Team was having a pre-Olympic camp in Chile, South America, and he told me that the best skier at that camp would get one World Cup start, in France. My first reaction: "Hell, no." I was excited about playing football and felt that the University of Colorado wanted me and the U.S. Ski Team did not. But Carroll challenged me to go so I could show the coaches how hard I had worked and how much better I was than everyone else. He told me that a sponsor would pay for my trip.

For a few days the challenge wore on my mind. There was no doubt that I was in the best shape of my life. I decided to go down there on a mission to prove a point. For the 22 days of the ski camp, I was the first one on the ski hill and the last one off. I was skiing top-to-bottom runs like my life depended on it. After each day, I would literally limp back to my apartment, soak in an ice bath for 20 minutes, and try to get myself ready for the next day. I was as hungry as ever to prove to my coaches that I was ready to become the best skier in the world.

I had to leave camp four days early to fly back for fall football camp in Colorado. The day before I was set to leave, U.S. Ski Team coaches Donnie St. Pierre, Liz McIntyre, and Scott Rawles asked to meet with me. We met in the lobby of the hotel in El Colorado, Chile. They looked me in the eye and told me that they had never seen anyone attack a training camp like I just had. They wanted to offer me one World Cup start in Tignes, France. If I finished in the top 12 there, I would be able to compete in every World Cup event leading up to the Olympics. It was an opportunity, although a small one. I had never placed in the top 12 of a World Cup race.

I flew back from Chile thinking about this situation the entire time. When I landed in Colorado, I called my mom and dad, and then I met with my football coach, Gary Barnett. I told Coach Barnett that I committed to play football this year and if he didn't want me to try to make the Olympic Ski Team, that I wouldn't do it, and I wouldn't think twice about the decision, even for a second.

Coach Barnett looked at me and told me something that I will never forget. He said, "Jeremy, I'm going to treat you like my son right now. I want you to go for your dream of becoming an Olympian; and your full-ride scholarship will be waiting for you here at CU next year. We will be cheering for you. Go make it happen."

I was so fired up, I was ready to run through a wall.

The next stop was Park City, Utah, to train full time with Chris Marchetti. He was introduced to me by my agent Andy Carroll, and training with him turned out to be one of the best decisions of my skiing career. We took our training to the next level. Sometimes I would wake up at 3 A.M. and hike a mountain because I knew my competitors were sleeping. It was intense, but I loved every second of it.

As the season approached, I felt nervous about having one shot to make the Olympic team. I flew to Tignes, France, for my first World Cup on the same day that the University of Colorado beat Texas to win the Big 12 title. I knew the pressure was on; not only did I turn away a chance to be part of a football team that just won a division title, but my dream of becoming an Olympian could be decided at this one competition.

In my qualification run, a big gust of wind covered the course with snow while I was skiing. The judges lost sight of me for a split second, so they made me take another run. That was a lucky break, because I had made a big mistake on that first run and would have never qualified for finals. In my next qualification run I told myself to let it loose. Don't hold back anything—a concept I've carried with me as I've built a company, too. My second run was much better and I qualified—in 12th place!

I couldn't believe it. I needed a top-12 finish to ski the rest of the World Cup and I qualified by ten one-hundredths of a point. You couldn't wipe the smile off my face if you tried. In the finals, I skied my heart out. I ended the event with a third place finish and qualified for the 2002 Olympic team!

While the 2002 Olympics didn't go as I had hoped, I ended the season as the number-one ranked skier in the world and won my first World Cup Overall Trophy. Over the next four years I won three world championships and 11 gold medals, and stood on the podium 26 times.

Back on Campus: A Football Dream Builds

As I arrived back on campus for my freshman football season, I did so with a national spotlight on me. It made me feel uncomfortable because as a freshman on a football team you don't want the attention on you; you want it on your team. To make things worse, the NCAA told me that they were not going to allow me to play college football and still get paid by my skiing sponsors. I decided to fight the NCAA in court over this decision, and that didn't exactly help remove the spotlight. I ended up losing my case and decided to forgo about $500,000 of skiing-related endorsement money to realize my dream of playing for the Colorado Buffaloes.

Many people called me foolish for turning away that type of money and told me that as a five-foot-nine, 175-pound receiver, I would never see the field. But I was confident in my ability, and I knew that I was the fastest guy on the field. As the season opened up against our in-state rivals Colorado State, I was not in the starting lineup as a receiver and was listed third on the punt return team. It was a tough three quarters. We were down 10–0 and couldn't seem to make anything work offensively.

As the third quarter ended, I heard Coach Barnett calling my name. I ran up to him and he said, "Jeremy, I want you to go return this punt." Without thinking, I said, "No problem," and grabbed my helmet. As

I started jogging onto the field, the moment hit me. I looked around and saw 80,000 people, national TV cameras, friends, and family in the stadium . . . and here I was returning a punt for my school.

All I could think was . . . "Don't drop the ball!"

The punt seemed to hang in the air forever, but as it came down, it did so right into my chest. I caught the ball, took two steps up the middle, then cut to the right sideline. I saw my ten teammates in front of me set up a perfect wall, and I raced down the sidelines. A few defenders missed me, and before I knew it, my hands were in the air and I was in the end zone. The first time I touched the ball in college football, I took a punt 75 yards to the house and scored a touchdown. I remember looking around seeing my teammates going crazy and fans jumping up and down and I thought to myself, "This is why I turned down that money." No amount of money could compare to that feeling.

For two years at college, I had the time of my life. I returned punts and played wide receiver for the Colorado Buffaloes. I set several school records, including the longest pass reception for a touchdown at 96 yards, and after my freshman season I was named First Team All American as a punt returner.

But I had a problem. There was still skiing and another Olympics was coming up. Yet, at this point I was broke. It was now 2004, and without the money I'd given up to play football, I would not be able to train for the 2006 Olympics. So I drew a line in the sand and told the NCAA that I was going to accept skiing-related endorsements so that I could train and compete for the United States in the next Olympics. I told them publicly that I was not leaving school, and if they didn't want me there, they would have to kick me out. They waited seven months to do so, and in August 2004, right before fall football camp opened, they declared me permanently ineligible.

I was incredibly upset. I couldn't understand why an organization would take something away from me that I had worked so hard for. But the decision was made, and there was nothing that I could do about it, so I packed my bags, left college, and began training for the Torino Olympics.

The Road to the NFL—and Beyond

Those of us on the U.S. Ski Team in Torino, Italy, were proud to represent our country. For me, however, it was more than that; it was a second chance to finish what I set out to do when I first watched skiing in the Olympics as a ten-year-old boy. Torino didn't turn out as I'd hoped, but I would not take the memory of that Olympic disappointment with me to the NFL Combine.

Or so I thought. It turned out my frustration in Torino was exactly what I needed as motivation to truly excel at the Combine. At the Combine there were more than 300 players ready to take part in a series of evaluations that include the 40-yard dash, 20-yard shuttle, vertical jump, broad jump, bench press, and position-specific drills along with injury evaluations, interviews, and more. For some players, it can help propel them higher up in the NFL draft. For others, like me, it can draw attention from scouts who might know your name but have not seen what you can do. I had been out of the action for two years at Colorado, so I needed to remind the NFL representatives what I was capable of on the field.

On April 30, 2006, two months after competing in Torino, I was selected by the Philadelphia Eagles in the fifth round of the NFL draft, the 147th selection overall.

I had gone from the Olympics to making it to the NFL in a few short months. I was on cloud nine. I spent two seasons with the Eagles and a season with the Pittsburgh Steelers. I had a blast playing in the NFL, sharing the locker room with guys like Donavan McNabb, Brian Dawkins, Ben Roethlisberger, Hines Ward, and Troy Polamalu. And it was incredible to be coached by legendary coaches such as Mike Tomlin and Andy Reid. While I would end up injuring my hamstring during training camp in 2008—ending my professional athletic career—I'd reached my goal of the NFL.

Now that my days as a professional athlete were over—all I focused on for so long—I worried about what life would be like for me after sports. I had ridden the waves from highs to lows and back up again, learning what it meant to be on a team as well as what it meant to stand on your own with everything riding on your shoulders.

I had been in the limelight, which was sometimes exciting, and other times overwhelming. Now I had my whole life ahead of me. What to do next? It would take time for me to figure that out.

But one thing was for sure—the failures I'd experienced would only serve to fuel whatever success I'd make for myself next.

CHAPTER TWO

MOVING FORWARD: THE 48-HOUR RULE

The night I failed to win a gold medal in the Olympics for the second time was one of the most painful nights of my life. I was heartbroken, angry, and confused. My dream of becoming an Olympic champion was over, and I didn't think I could find any way to snap out of it. But as I wrestled with the pain and the deluge of emotions, I made a pact with myself. I would allow myself 48 hours to obsess over everything that had happened—and then I was going to completely move on and not look back.

If you're going to succeed, you cannot dwell on defeat or missed opportunities, and you can't allow them to define you. I've found that to be true for both sports and business.

When it comes to dealing with adversity, John Maxwell describes how people deal with negative situations in his book *The Difference Maker*: "I've found that there are really only two kinds of people in this world when it comes to dealing with discouragement: splatters and bouncers. When splatters hit rock bottom, they fall apart, and they stick to the bottom like glue. On the other hand, when bouncers hit bottom, they pull together and bounce back."

The most evolved bouncers I know hit rock bottom, methodically dissect what happened, resist the urge to allow the loss to define them, and decipher learning to refine their road map for success. Although certain personality traits are characteristic of a bouncer or a splatter, the good news is that understanding how to constructively deal with adversity is a learned skill, not something that you are born with.

Much of what I discuss in this book is designed to provoke thoughts and ideas to arm you with the skills and insights necessary to improve your ability to constructively deal with adversity.

The Power of Deadlines

The most important step to overcoming adversity and negative feelings: Don't wallow. Instead, set a deadline for accepting what has happened, at least emotionally. This emotional acceptance stage is crucial—and so is the deadline.

This stage is defined by the amount of time it takes for you to accept your new reality. You'll have to give yourself a deadline for getting through this period.

During this time you will take these steps:

1. Replay what took place in your mind.
2. Go through emotional phases that will likely include despair, anguish, anger, and a desire to retaliate. Allow yourself to feel these emotions and try not to hold back.
3. Examine what went wrong prior to the failure or defeat and consider what signs you may have missed that might have led to failure.
4. Look at what you could do differently in the future.

The third and fourth points on this list are critical. Examining what went wrong can take two paths. The first path looks back and leads you to understand what contributed to your failure. Was there a flaw in your preparation? Did you lose focus? Were you distracted by outside noise or doubt? Were you mentally prepared? Did you feel too much pressure? For athletes, there's also the question of training hard enough and getting enough sleep.

The second path leads you down the road ahead to what you can do differently next time. Areas you identify as contributing to a failure inevitably can be improved upon, and understanding what contributed to the negative outcome is a key to getting a better result. During this time, I ask myself: "What did I learn in this experience that I can apply next time?" I try to imagine myself in the same situation and think about how I might prepare for it differently or how I might act on opportunities or react to specific obstacles.

Then I take what I've learned and I move on. It's very important to set a defined deadline for yourself to move past this stage. In life we are surrounded by deadlines, whether it's for completing homework, earning a spot on a team, passing an audition, filing our taxes, or completing a business deal. Some deadlines are outside our control, while others, if we are honest with ourselves, are of our own making. Limiting the time that we allow things to consume us strengthens our ability to control our thoughts and actions.

That is the key to using failures to fuel your successes. Setting deadlines for dwelling on failures can play a major role in whether we succeeded at our future goals, or even go after them in the first place.

Setting a deadline gives us:

▷ Practice for disciplined control over our minds;
▷ Something to look forward to;
▷ A sense of resolve.

48 Hours—and That's It

After leaving Torino in 2006, I headed straight for the NFL Combine. I was devastated, but I had to put everything that happened into perspective—and I had to do so quickly if I wanted to give myself the best opportunity to fulfill my dream of getting drafted into the NFL. It was during that transition from the end of my skiing dreams to pursuing my quest to fulfill my football dreams that I developed the 48-hour rule to get over major disappointments.

Earlier in my career, mistakes or disappointments would sometimes weigh too heavily on me and stay with me for a very long time. They were difficult to shake and caused me to lose focus and concentration. I needed to develop a consistent structure and process for dealing with disappointment to effectively learn from my mistakes and keep moving. It's the same in business, where losing a client or a big deal can sit with you and actually make it harder to win that next client or deal.

During my 48 hours, I gave myself freedom to feel the loss, to express the emotion, to attach to the behaviors, to roll it over in my head time and time again, and to sequester myself from the outside world to deal with everything that I had just experienced. After the 48-hour window was up, I committed myself 100 percent to moving on.

How Much Time Do You Need?

Of course we are not all alike, so how long you need to recover might be different. Not every failure or disappointment is so big that you need 48 hours to process it, while some might be much bigger and need much more time—and sometimes, you simply don't have the luxury of that much time. It's healthy to employ a variety of time frames, depending on the severity of the experience. For example, if I lose a client I'll give myself an hour to deal with it, put together a go-forward plan that includes ideas on how to get them back, and then leave any feelings of lost confidence behind. For moments of adversity like the Olympics, I allow myself the full 48 hours. However, for someone else it might be 96 hours or even a couple of months or more.

The time you'll need is predicated largely on three factors:

1. Significance of your goal
2. Time invested

3. Having another goal, or several other goals

People who have invested every dollar of their personal capital in a business venture only to see it crumble may very well take more time to move on than someone who started a company on a whim. The same holds true in our personal life, where it's typically much easier to get over a dating relationship that lasted a few months than to get through a painful divorce after 20 years of marriage. And, of course, having another big goal (for me, the NFL) makes it somewhat easier to set shorter time frames for getting past a failure.

My challenge to you is to set shorter deadlines. It will feel uncomfortable and unnatural, but you need to work your way through the process without taking too much time to dwell or fall back into negativity.

Three Mental Keys

When I won my first World Championship gold medal in skiing, I employed three mental points of focus: to keep my mind like a river, live downstairs, and focus on my skills. Here's how they work.

Mind Like a River

The concept of "mind like a river" was one that I came up with after all the times I knew I made a mistake because I hadn't been able to get rid of a self-defeating thought that was trapped in my mind. One time I was competing in a World Cup, and I had qualified in first place, which means that you are the last person to ski in the finals. A skier who I did not like was winning the competition, and if I didn't have a great run, he was going to win. I hated the idea of this guy winning, and all I could think about was him winning his first World Cup—and not wanting that to happen. As I approached the top jump, I was more focused on beating him than on what I needed to do to land the trick. I landed on my back and finished last. Other times, I would be in the starting gate and a thought would pop into my mind, such as: "I am going to crash," or "I didn't prepare well enough," or "My legs don't feel good," or "The score is too high to beat."

Self-defeating thoughts are very normal; almost everyone has them. They might come up just before a big business pitch, a company presentation, media interviews, or a critical meeting. You need to have a game plan for how you are going to deal with them.

For me, I decided to make my mind like a river. It was a simple, but powerful idea that I could also "see" in my mind's eye. I would picture a fast-moving river flowing through the back of my head and out the front. No thought could stick in this fast-moving current. This took a lot of practice and mastering—it didn't happen overnight—but it was one of the best mental skills that I ever learned.

For someone else it might be releasing the momentary disappointment or frustration into an imaginary balloon sailing off into the wind, so it simply blows away. The point is, you need a strong visual image of something that will move the emotions away from you. Visualize putting them in a bottle, and tossing that into the ocean.

Using such mental imagery is also very successful when you need to react quickly. We don't always have 48 hours to come to terms with adversity. For example, if a goalie in hockey or soccer holds onto the negative feelings about the goal he just gave up, he is more likely to give up another one. If I dropped a pass in football and did not let the bad feeling that came with that flow out of my mind, I knew I would be more likely to drop another one. Why? Because holding onto the negative thoughts about the previous play would make me doubt myself. Athletes cannot dwell on an error or mistake as the game continues. They must regain focus quickly. This is also the case in business. Consider a stockbroker making trades in the market. He simply cannot let a drop in the market eat him up or he will miss the opportunities to jump back in and make profitable trades—sometimes trades that need to be made moments after a big loss.

Living Downstairs

The second skill that I attempted to master was a concept that I created called "living downstairs." We all encounter distractions that we can't control, and many of them put enormous pressure on us—but only if we allow them to. In my athletic career these outside pressures included knowing my parents were traveling halfway around the world to watch me compete, a nationally televised event, *Sports Illustrated* picking me to win, a girl that I was trying to impress, and more.

In business these distractions often include fear of letting down employees, noise from a competitor, or a naysayer trying to break your confidence, among other things. At times when I really need to focus but am facing a lot of outside noise, I close my eyes and picture myself walking downstairs into a cold, windowless cellar where no outside thoughts can get in. And if those thoughts ever pierced the cellar of my mind, I would simply picture a fast-moving river carrying them away immediately.

For you, living downstairs might mean creating a space below the big-picture thoughts, pressures, and distractions. It provides a safe space. Maybe for you it's upstairs above the grinding news of the day to day. Whatever it might be, create a mental space where there are no windows or doors so that once your mind is clear, you can focus on your tasks and goals.

Focus on Your Skills

The third concept I relied on was to "focus on the skills." This was a concept that I learned from former U.S. Olympic Ski Team coach Cooper Schell, who successfully coached American Jonny Moseley to a gold medal at the 1998 Nagano Olympics. Schell taught me that no matter what situation I was in, I could always come back to my skills. I knew in my mind that I had worked harder and longer than any of my competitors to master the skills necessary to be best in the world, so this idea gave me more confidence. In skiing, that meant reminding myself that my skills would get me down the mountain 100 percent of the time. In football it was remembering that my skills would allow me to catch every ball, punt, and kickoff.

We all go through periods in life where we feel a little lost. When you do, always come back to what you know and have the confidence to trust in your skills. In business, that could mean reminding yourself that your skills as a salesman will allow you to clinch a deal, or that your skills as a marketer will give you what you need to create a successful campaign, or that your financial acumen will allow you to budget just right every time.

EVEN-KEELED

As the old saying goes, "Don't allow the good days to go to your head or the bad days to go to your heart."

One characteristic that I have found shared by the most successful people I know is their ability to stay even-keeled through the highs and the lows of life, business, and sport. John Elway is one of those people. Although he'd been a hero of mine, I didn't meet him until he was thinking about bringing an arena league football team to Denver. He wanted my thoughts on how to make the team relevant to young people. After getting to know Elway over the next several years, it became obvious to me that his success in athletics and business had a lot to do with his calm mind and even temperament.

During his 16 seasons as an NFL quarterback, and even today as a general manager and executive vice president of football operations for the Denver Broncos, Elway has always remained even-keeled. Sure, he's had his triumphant moments and his disappointments, but one of the things that always impressed me was his approach to the game. He never seemed unnerved or shaken by what occurred on the field. He had the head for the game and a disposition that kept him under control.

I'm the type of person who wears my emotions on my sleeve, so it has been a challenge for me to evolve into someone who can keep his emotions in check. I have not come close to mastering this skill, but it is something that I have improved on. And in doing so, I have become more consistent and prepared in almost everything I encounter.

Passion, Resiliency, and Steve Jobs

Once you've mastered these three keys, you can put your passion and resiliency to work.

Steve Jobs provides an inspiring story of passion, resiliency, and tenacity. His 2005 speech to the graduating class of Stanford University is one of my favorite keynotes. In it, Jobs, who never graduated from college, talked about the ten-year journey he had taken with his business partner, Steve Wozniak, from a small business in a garage to a $2 billion company with more than 4,000 employees. Passionate about their work, they had succeeded in creating Apple and had released the Macintosh. They were elated. Then, about a year later, Jobs was fired from the company he had founded.

During the commencement speech, he asked the question: "How can you get fired from a company you started?" It does baffle the mind. However, I see it happen all the time.

"What had been the focus of my entire adult life was gone, and it was devastating," said Jobs about walking away from his passion. For some time, Jobs felt the pain and guilt of letting others down. He even apologized for "screwing up."

It was shortly thereafter, though, that Jobs realized that he had lost his position at Apple, but he had not lost his passion. He would refocus and move forward. "I didn't see it then, but it turned out that getting fired from Apple was the best thing that could have ever happened to me," he says. "The heaviness of being successful was replaced by the lightness of being a beginner again, less sure about everything. It freed me to enter one of the most creative periods of my life."

He moved forward and started NeXT Computer, Inc. and NeXT Software, Inc., and then moved on to launch Pixar Animation Studios. Today, Pixar is one of the most successful animation studios on the planet. And Jobs eventually came back to Apple, reviving the company and overseeing the development of the iPod, iPhone, and iPad.

"Sometimes life hits you in the head with a brick.
Don't lose faith."
—STEVE JOBS

I can't say how long it took Jobs to rebound from being fired from his own company, but like others who are steadfast in their desire to succeed, he rebounded quickly. Moving beyond the disappointment does not mean losing your passions, but reprogramming them. Most significantly, it means getting on with life and no longer dwelling on something that has already occurred.

Bill Buckner will probably never forget letting the ground ball slip through his legs—the play that prevented the Boston Red Sox from winning the 1986 World Series. But these days, Buckner signs autographs for fans alongside the very guy who hit the ball, Mookie Wilson.

It's part of his life and he has wrapped his mind around it and even used it to his advantage. You can be sure that superstar entrepreneur Sir Richard Branson, of Virgin Airlines and Virgin Records fame and fortune, can tell you all about Virgin Cola and Virgin Vodka, since he moved on from those failed ideas but never lost his drive for success.

Planting Seeds

Of course you might think it's easier to use the 48-hour rule and bounce back when you have another goal waiting in the wings, like my goal of making the NFL. And you know what? You're right.

Planting seeds in other areas has always been part of my long-term strategy. Doing things actively to invest in your future is just a very smart thing to do. Too many people put all their eggs in one basket, as the saying goes. They have one goal, one dream, and one pursuit for better or worse. I can't count the number of times growing up that I heard I should only focus on skiing because I was too small to play football and that I might have a better shot at getting to the Olympics if I maintained a single focus. Some coaches wanted me to specialize when I was as young as 12 years old! I didn't listen—and I'm happy that I didn't.

Gary Barnett, my football coach at the University of Colorado, used to tell me to "never leave a stone unturned." That is something I have tried to always adhere to.

I planted a lot of seeds in a lot of different areas throughout my athletic career. Most of them did not grow, but they all taught me some important lessons, and I got to meet some very interesting people along the way. It was having a variety of goals that led me to where I am now, my role as the CEO of Integrate and founder of Wish of a Lifetime. However, each of us only has so much bandwidth, and you need to be careful how much time you dedicate to investing in your future if you're currently attacking a goal. I think a good rule of thumb is about 5 percent of your time—devote that amount to planting future seeds you can grow if your current plans fall flat.

Eliminating Distractions

There are strategic times in life when you need to close off all distractions and focus on one goal. The United States Olympic Committee commissioned a report on what the most common distractions were for Olympians competing in the games. By far, the number-one distraction for many athletes has to do with family members. Families traveled across the world to see their athlete compete, and they would often request tickets or want to spend time with them the nights leading up to the competition.

Because of this, I would turn my cell phone off for the three weeks leading up to the competition and had a game plan with all family members that included no contact until after my competition. I'd shut off my emails and set up a new email address for only a few people. This was all part of my "distraction elimination plan," and it worked. I never felt distracted by family, friends, or acquaintances while competing at the games.

In business I have also had occasions where my mental bandwidth had to be so focused on specific activities that I became unable to respond to people or even to be with my family. Everyone needs to work on and master his or her own work-life integration plan.

Today, I spend most of my time at Integrate, but I am also at my nonprofit, Wish of a Lifetime, that has a mission of granting life-enriching wishes to some of the oldest people in our society. While I am passionately dedicated to both, I know that I cannot be in both places at once, so I have hired people to run the day-to-day operations at the nonprofit. Yet when it comes to a major decision or an important fundraiser, I am 100 percent mentally present because of my passion for the nonprofit and my goal to see it succeed.

KEEPING FOCUS

The two most important actions to take in order to stay mentally focused are:

1. Eliminate the outside noise.

2. Focus on what you want to master.

CHAPTER THREE

DEFINING FAILURE

There was nothing in the world that I wanted to do more than win an Olympic gold medal. The thought of standing on top of the podium, watching the American flag being raised, and hearing the national anthem play gave me chills. I was 19 years old, the number-one ranked skier in the world, and the Olympics were being hosted in my home country.

With almost every one of my family members in attendance, I finished in ninth place.

It was the first time I'd ever experienced this kind of loss. I didn't know how to handle it, how to learn from it, or how to move past it. I certainly didn't know how to embrace it—at least not yet.

What Is Failure?

Webster's dictionary defines failure as "the nonperformance of an assigned or expected action" or "a falling short of one's goals." I consider the first definition to apply to the short-term failures that we all experience often when trying to do something, such as missing a sales quota for the quarter. The second definition, however, has far greater impact on us since our goals can be very closely tied to who we are as individuals.

The fact that there is an inherent fear of even the mention of the word *failure* was part of what ultimately led me to write this book. "I even avoid using that word *failure*, as it seems to have such a negative

LEARNING FROM LOSING

Former NFL quarterback Fran Tarkenton has his own philosophies about winning and losing, some of which he has shared in his book *What Losing Taught Me About Winning*.

In an Entrepreneur.com article by Tarkenton, "4 Success Strategies I Took from the NFL to My Business," he writes: "Losing a game taught me so much more than winning one. When we won, the team went out to dinner with our families. We talked, laughed, and reminisced about the game, the plays, and even a fumble or two. But the team didn't go out when we lost. I went home and studied. I watched film. I needed to understand what went wrong and how I could have played better to change the outcome. I applied my learning to our next practice and game, which helped me constantly improve."

Tarkenton, who today runs Tarkenton Companies, a financial firm that is focused on small-business and retirement solutions, also believes that failure is not a bad thing if you learn to "identify and quantify a failure before it compounds itself over time."

connotation," Karen Cogan, senior sports psychologist for the United States Olympic Committee, tells me. I worked with Karen during my ski career and she helped me a lot during those years. She also says, "For some athletes, if they make an Olympic team, that's the most amazing accomplishment ever, but for others, if they don't get the gold medal at the Olympics they feel that they have failed, so the definition of failure is going to vary greatly. It's a very personal thing and each person defines their own idea of success and failure."

Whatever that definition is, when you lose, you will need time and space to put it into proper perspective. With athletes, Karen tries to "focus on the positive things they have accomplished, but it often takes time before they can separate themselves from the unattained goal and see such accomplishments." I know that was the case for me.

Of course, most people do not start out thinking of, or defining, failure. They start on the opposite track, by considering what success means to them. And even the definition of success differs depending on many factors. We are influenced by our families, our peers, our culture, and more. For me, success was initially tied to athletics. I saw victories in sports as success, and that was what I wanted more than anything else. Starting at a young age, success meant winning on the slopes or the football field.

The Ways We Fail

There are actually plenty of ways to fail. I was surprised to find out there's at least one person who actually studies failure, since most people spend more time thinking about what makes us successful. Management, strategy, and leadership professor Sydney Finkelstein of Dartmouth College's Tuck School of Business has a fascinating view of failure—he even wrote a book about it (*Why Smart Executives Fail*). I asked Professor Finkelstein to help me explain failure, and one of his first insights—one I find true in my own life—is that while there may be only a limited number of ways in which to succeed, there are many ways to fail.

"Having a bad idea, not executing well, not having the courage to change or adapt, not building the right team, or making bad decisions are among so many possible ways in which we can fail," Professor Finkelstein tells me. Another way of failing: not even trying.

There are more typical, tangible ways that we fail that are defined by the world around us. "The consequences of failure in a company are big. You can lose your job, for one. Or if you're in school and don't perform up to par, you might not graduate," Professor Finkelstein explains. But a lot of things in life are hard—they might even seem insurmountable, especially if you've already experienced a setback or failure. "Many people become scared of failure and not only do not want to embrace it, but often stop putting themselves out there," Professor Finkelstein says. "Since we all have a desire to feel good about ourselves, when we fail at something and don't feel good about ourselves, we feel there is something wrong . . . failure doesn't help our self-image. Then we become less confident and we may fail to try new things or to take bigger risks."

The bottom line: Failure builds. Failure can lead to more failure. That is, unless you learn to use each failure to your advantage, to let it fuel your future success.

The Weight of Failure

The loftiness of one's goals makes not achieving them harder to deal with. In many ways, reaching for stars is no different from the risk-and-reward factors investing gurus and financial planners talk about. The greater the risk, the greater the potential rewards. The flip side is the greater the risk, the greater the potential losses.

Olympic athletes, for example, take very big risks. They put so much of their lives into preparing that when things don't go the way they hoped, they can end up feeling devastated. It's something my sports psychologist saw a lot of, too. "I've seen instances where it can take years to come to terms with failing to win a medal, or in some cases, the gold medal," Karen Cogan tells me. "And even then, after a couple of years, there's still this horrible memory of what happened as those athletes are reliving it again and again, beating themselves up over having done something wrong."

IT'S NOT GIVING UP, IT'S REFOCUSING

How many failures does it take before it's time to refocus one's goals? Here too, the answer will differ greatly depending on whom you ask. Examples abound across the spectrum. There are those who took their LSATs for law school admission once, received a score that was too low to get into a good law school, and never tried again. There are people who tried out for the football team as a freshman in high school, didn't make it, and never returned to try again as a sophomore.

There are many people who started a small business that failed, never to try again, even if the failure was simply a matter of circumstance and had little to do with the person's ability to manage a business or generate good ideas.

"Failure can make you scared to try again or to take a risk," Professor Finkelstein reminds us. The weight of having failed can cause people to give up quickly.

Conversely, people on the other end of the spectrum don't take failure to heart. Consider actors who've auditioned for many roles over the years with very little or no success; serial entrepreneurs who've watched five, six, or seven businesses go belly-up; and athletes who hang around the minor leagues until they are older than 30 without making it to the major leagues. These are people who can't acknowledge that they failed at a goal or dream, so they keep trying, when in reality they are failing to learn from their experiences.

When I left sports, I recognized where I had succeeded, which made me feel great. But I was also able to come to terms with goals I had failed to achieve. Doing so allowed me to refocus my goals and move on to my post-sports career.

Getting past such a failure is a process that, like grieving, takes time. The more you invest, the harder it is to recover and the more the failure will weigh on you.

"In a minor competition, sure, athletes are disappointed at the loss or mistakes they may have made, but they can typically go right back out there and try again in the next competition," Karen says. "There are more chances to succeed right around the corner, with the next tennis match or tournament only days or weeks away. But when it's the Olympics, it's four years of waiting before the next chance comes and for most athletes that feels like eternity."

Embracing Failure to Succeed in Business

The more time and money invested to start a company, the longer it can take an entrepreneur to assess what went wrong and process the failure. That's traditional thinking. And, while it has been true in many cases, and many entrepreneurs do take a much-needed break to refuel before getting back in the game, others are able to rebound quickly.

Today, thanks largely to tech web-based businesses, many entrepreneurs can revive their businesses or start over more quickly than brick-and-mortar locations. It's also easier to reach out to identify investors through the internet and the rapid nature of word-of-mouth communication. That can make it easier to bounce back from failure for some internet-based entrepreneurs.

What would you do if you saw your entire business shut down suddenly? That's what happened to PYP Media's Kathryn Minshew. The web-based career resource for young women shut down in 2011 following major disagreements between PYP's other cofounders. Kathryn had poured her entire life savings, $20,000, into the business and had nothing left to show for it. But rather than wallow in the failed business, Kathryn and some of her team from PYP decided to dust themselves off and dive into a new venture, The MUSE, a far more successful career website of which Kathryn is now CEO.

Sometimes, it takes a little longer to bounce right back. When Christina Wallace and her partner shut down their business, Quincy

Apparel, she climbed into bed and pulled up the covers. "After 21 days of sleeping and crying, I put on my big-girl pants and rejoined the world," says Christina, who is now vice president of branding and marketing at Startup Institute, a career accelerator that helps people working in startups become more successful.

The point is, failure can weigh heavily on people, but each of us reacts in a different way. That doesn't mean it's wrong to take more time. It only means that at some point, you need to put your failure aside and get back in the game.

Admitting Failure

Being able to admit you failed at something is a liberating experience. Yet one of the hardest things to say is, "I failed." But by admitting it, you've literally set yourself free of the weight of it.

The trouble is, people will go to great lengths to lie to themselves and to others to avoid admitting failure. Politicians make a career out of dodging their failures and stay in office. Some people create an endless stream of excuses or look for someone to blame for their failures rather than owning up to them.

The real reason admitting failure is so hard? It makes us feel very vulnerable. Saying "I failed" means dropping your guard and opening yourself up to criticism or self-deprecation. It also may mean giving up on a goal or a dream because you feel like you've let down your family, friends, colleagues, or fans.

What we often forget is that our perception of failure primarily comes from ourselves, our parents, our culture, our perception of the world, our financial situation, where we grow up, and what we see and hear from the media. There are so many things telling us what failure and success are supposed to look like. Our views get clouded and we forget that really, it's all relative.

> *"If you set your goal ridiculously high and it's a failure, you will fail above everyone else's success."*
>
> —JAMES CAMERON

Why We're So Afraid to Embrace Failure

If admitting failure makes you uncomfortable, actually embracing it can be nearly impossible. We learn from an early age that failure is bad, so why would we want to embrace it?

First, it's important to understand that you can embrace failure in a negative or a positive way. There are many people who see embracing failure as negative or a sign of weakness. They will try to keep their failures hidden like the man behind the curtain in *The Wizard of Oz*. They believe that by embracing failure, they are giving up, giving in, or setting up much lower standards. Defining yourself as a failure is another negative way of embracing it. It is an excuse to say, "I can't do it," "I give up," or "Why bother, I won't succeed anyway . . . I will therefore settle for less or for something that does not satisfy me."

What people who see failure this way do not recognize is that sometimes you need to go back to the base of the mountain to start climbing again.

FAILURE GOES COMMERCIAL

You may have heard of Comic-Con, the annual event in cities such as San Diego and New York that brings together aficionados of comic books, games, sci-fi, and related pop culture. Well, now there is FailCon, a global one-day event to help tech entrepreneurs, investors, developers, and designers transition from a fear of failure to embracing it. Attendees in the United States, Spain, Japan, Brazil, France, Iran, and the United Arab Emirates gather to share their stories of business startups gone wrong, plans that didn't work, bad hires, sales predictions that missed the mark, and so forth.

The idea of FailCon, which started in San Francisco in 2009, is to let people know that it is okay to fail, it's part of life, and that you can go right back out there and build something bigger and better the next time if you acknowledge having failed and move on.

Embracing Failure in a Positive Way

Embracing failure positively requires a leap of faith, but once you jump over the hurdle, you will understand that fearing failure only holds you back from realizing your full potential.

Eric Roza, CEO of Datalogix, whose story of failure and success comes up later in Chapter 5, says that at his company, the corporate culture practically encourages people to acknowledge their failures or errors at monthly company meetings via a "Stay Humble, Keep Improving" moment.

"By acknowledging it as a group, we can all fail and that is okay," Eric told me when I asked him why he does this. I met Eric through a coworker, the CFO of Integrate David Tomizuka in 2013 and we became fast friends. By recognizing that everyone fails, the people at Datalogix are able to embrace it as a regular part of life. Since most of what we learn is from trial and error, beginning when we fall down again and again trying to walk, it's only natural to recognize that everyone fails . . . often.

FIVE WAYS EMBRACING FAILURE CAN WORK FOR YOU

1. We learn some of our best lessons through failure.

2. Failure inspires us. If we look at it properly and don't allow it to define us, failure can be a great source of motivation.

3. Failure teaches us humility. We feel humble after losing and recognize that we are indeed human.

4. Embracing failure allows us to take more risks. Once we come to terms with having failed and survived, we can take greater risks.

5. Failure makes success taste even better. We have a better appreciation of success having failed a few times on the way up the ladder.

"Once you have embraced failure, you no longer fear it," Eric says.

That echoes what I've always thought about letting failure fuel you—and Professor Finkelstein sums it up pretty simply: "That's the point of embracing failure in a positive way . . . it allows you to move past the negatives and the disappointments and change your mindset from 'failure is bad' to 'failure can be good and here's how to make it a tool for you.'"

If you don't constructively embrace failure in a healthy way, you'll get stuck and won't allow yourself to accomplish what you could. The importance of separating yourself from having failed, reprogramming your ego, and walking away with a new plan are the themes carried out in the rest of this book.

CHAPTER FOUR

FORGET WINNING:
REPROGRAM YOUR EGO

Is winning everything? For me it was . . . for a very long time. After all, I was born into a culture and media landscape that taught me that my heroes should be those with the most wins, people who make the most money and attract the most fame.

I wanted to win everything, beat every skier on the mountain, win every football game in which I played, and be the best player in the world. My concept of winning was defined by what I saw around me, the perks of being a winner. And then, I lost.

Being focused on winning isn't necessarily bad. On one hand, it is healthy to be driven to succeed at whatever you do. And let's face it, winning feels amazing. My desire to win helped me in many ways, driving me to train longer, harder, and more intensely than I ever thought possible. My former athletic trainer, Chris Marchetti, would tell people that my biggest blind spot as an athlete was that I consistently overtrained. I wouldn't give my body a chance to recuperate because I was obsessed with having the mental confidence of knowing that I worked harder than everyone else.

Above all, being ego-driven is not a bad thing if your ego is fed by the right sources of motivation. I have learned that motivation has to come from within. It has to be your innate, internal desire and not something imposed by the outside world. Those external motivators are in large part why we have a hard time getting over our failures: We measure ourselves too much by what others have to say.

The big question, therefore, is: How should we define success? Is it defined by external motivating factors, as it was for me, or can it be formed by intrinsic motivating factors, as it later became for me? You can overcome failure—use it to inspire you, even—when you shift your motivation. But to do that, you'll first have to reprogram your ego.

When Your Ego Gets in Your Way

If you define your self-worth by how you stack up to other people, you will never reach your full potential or enjoy a happy life. Consistently measuring your success against someone else's accomplishments is treadmill goal-setting. Trust me, this is a race you will never win, and you'll be left feeling like you're forever running on a treadmill chasing an unattainable goal.

Remember the story that I told in Chapter 2 about how I let my need to beat a skier that I didn't like dominate my thought process instead of focusing on my skills? My ego got the best of me that day, but it was the beginning of what would become one of the most important lessons I have ever learned.

In the fall of 2004, my mom gave me a book by Wayne Dyer called *The Power of Intention*. Shortly after flying to South America to train for the World Cup season, I opened the book and dove in. I came to a section of the book where Dyer talked about giving up the need to win. My first reaction was, "Ha, ha, this guy has lost his mind!" Why would

I give up my need to win? That's what defined my life, motivated me to get this far—it was the foundation of my entire athletic career.

But the statement stuck with me. It kept me up at night, and I found myself coming back to it time and time again. I started to unpack the thought in my head and began questioning whether my desire to win was actually hurting my ability to in fact win. I reflected back on my athletic career and on my wins and my losses along the way. I realized that I was an extrinsically motivated person. All I cared about was beating so-and-so, having everyone like me, making money, and getting attention.

After digesting this self-revelation, I became obsessed with figuring out ways to remove the motivational control that my ego had on my goals.

But how can you take 22 years of social conditioning and completely reprogram your ego? I started by doing something that made me uncomfortable: helping my biggest competitors. In training, I would mention tips for the course, things like, "Hey, watch out for the last turn before the top jump, it's sharp and icy . . . take it high left and you will be fine." This became one of the most liberating things that I had ever experienced. I wasn't trying to help them win, but I stopped thinking about who I needed to beat. Instead I replaced that externally focused mental bandwidth with thoughts of how I could get better every single day. Pat Riley, former coach of the New York Knicks and current president of the Miami Heat, has summed it up eloquently: "A champion needs a motivation above and beyond winning." Another Riley sentiment also resonates: "Excellence is the gradual result of always striving to do better."

It is not uncommon to find yourself focusing on beating someone, to your own detriment. In sports, one of the most egregious examples of ego-driven career destruction came from Olympic figure skater Tanya Harding. At the 1994 U.S. Figure Skating Championships, she was linked to a physical attack on her rival Nancy Kerrigan. The attack took Kerrigan out of the competition. It was one of the biggest news stories of the year and the beginning of the end of the skating career of Harding, a former U.S. champion who went on to finish eighth in the 1994 Olympics and was later banned from competition.

The CEO Ego

Businesses can also become ego-driven when CEOs and decision-makers stick to paths that don't keep up with changing trends or competition. On June 19, 2012, one of the most iconic companies in history filed for bankruptcy. Kodak, which has traces dating all the way back to 1880, failed to innovate quickly enough in the digital camera revolution and ultimately lost most of its market share to companies like Canon and Sony.

For some athletes, as well as businesspeople and entertainers, ego gets in the way when they start reading and believing the headlines written about them. It's easy to become obsessed with every word that is written, and you easily get discouraged when an article doesn't paint a perfect picture of you. This is a dangerous game. Soon, you spend more time thinking about what was written about you than focusing on getting better every day.

Today, everyone has a microphone. With the popularity of social media, anyone, anywhere can state their opinion publicly in a forum that is easily searchable. The praise or criticism can cause your self-esteem to go up or down like a stock in the market if you let it. Failures and successes in life can be magnified to the point where they can distort the image you have of yourself.

I used to be the biggest offender when it came to reading my own headlines. I would try to read everything that was written about me. I learned that there was really no upside. The nice comments felt normal, but the bad things brought me down. For many people, the ego is fed by one particular extrinsic factor, the desire to have everyone like you. And that's impossible.

A fellow athlete at the Olympics once told me: "I don't know the key to success, but the key to failure is trying to please everyone."

Letting Go of the Need to Win

To become more intrinsically motivated, I stopped focusing on beating others, getting rich, and caring what everyone thought about me. I began to focus more on what I wanted to get out of life, the person that

I ultimately wanted to become, and how I could get better at whatever I was doing. And ironically, I started winning much more often.

Sometimes we get stuck analyzing and thinking under a microscope. It's healthy at times to zoom up a few levels and look through the telescope. It's also important to focus on enjoying what you do. If you are passionate about something, as I was about skiing and football, or as I am today about my business and my nonprofit, you want to let yourself get in touch with the part of you that truly gets pleasure from what you are doing.

Part of what helped me make the shift to intrinsic motivation was reflecting on my early love of skiing. As I mentioned, I grew up skiing with my family. We did it together and it was fun. There were no medals to be won or awards handed out when my family hit the slopes. It was all about our passion for skiing. I wanted to recapture that.

In time, I began to embrace the philosophy of intrinsic motivation. I took on the idea of skiing just for me and I found that I was improving because I wanted to be the best skier I could possibly be, not the skier who beat so-and-so. I no longer compared myself to others or concerned myself with what the competition was doing. It was about winning for me, which is the greatest motivation.

Granted, this doesn't happen overnight, even when you're motivated to change. It took me some time to make the transition. It felt unnatural at first. It was sort of like learning another language and then trying to speak in that language. But gradually, I stopped thinking about everyone else and started honing in on what mattered to me alone—skiing up to my potential.

I remember the moment it really all came together. It was in Deer Valley, Utah, at a World Cup in 2005. It was the third World Cup of the year, and in the previous two I had gotten terrible results. However, I knew that I was very close to mastering the skills that I was working on. Everything clicked and I won that day—by a wide margin.

But the feeling was different. I wasn't excited because I beat other people; I was completely fulfilled because I skied the very best run that I could. I put everything that I had been working on the past year together. When I won my second consecutive World Cup event the next day, I felt like I was skiing to my potential and I had a feeling that I wouldn't lose the rest of the year. I had complete mental clarity and my ego no longer had any effect on my preparation or focus. When I won my fourth and fifth consecutive World Cup events, more and more people began approaching me to talk about setting a new record in the sport. Winning a sixth event would break the record.

Once upon a time I would have completely attached to that and it would have made me nervous. I would have thought to myself, here is my chance to make history. I must win. But instead, I found it rather annoying. I still thought it would be cool to set a record, but more so because it would mean that I once again accomplished my goal of skiing up to my potential.

I had read Wayne Dyer's book in early 2005 and proceeded, that year, to reprogram my ego, drown out the extrinsic noise, and self-motivate. As a result, in 2005, I won nine World Cup events, including a record-setting six in a row. People often ask how athletes get in "the zone." Reprogramming my ego to focus intrinsically was how I did it.

It's Not Black and White

Without the proper practice and wisdom, it can be very hard not to compare ourselves to others. And, of course, it's easy to focus on the idea that we want to beat our opponents in sport or business. There's nothing wrong with competition. But you need to ask yourself: What is my motivation? Is it the love of the fame and attention or the love of the mission?

Can you be totally intrinsically motivated?

"Not necessarily, it's not always black and white," says Brad Feld, partner at the Boulder, Colorado-based venture capital firm Foundry Group. I consider Brad a good friend and an expert at understanding the difference between intrinsic and extrinsic motivation. I met Brad through a good friend, Bing Gordon, the founder of EA Sports, and we quickly became friends. As he explains, "People fall along a continuum."

Brad uses tennis star Rafael Nadal as an example. He sees Nadal as having a blend of both extrinsic and intrinsic motivation. Nadal clearly likes to win. He likes the limelight and the attention he gets. "Yet . . .

Nadal, after he loses a match, he's a very gracious loser, acknowledging that the other guy played better and did an awesome job," Brad explained to me.

Nadal recharges his battery by heading off to the beach, and then he is back in training for the next tournament. His daily training regime includes four hours of playing tennis on court, two and a half hours in the gym, and a strict stretching routine. He's continued this training whether he is ranked at number one, five, or seven in the world. It's for him, not for the ranking.

Brad also believes something I've really taken to heart—that one person can't truly motivate another person, a concept especially important in business when you manage people. "I can't motivate another person, but [I can] create a context in which they are motivated, and part of being a leader is to understand what motivates other people," explained Brad. "So if I'm the leader of an organization that you're a part of, I have to understand what motivates you. Then I can create a context in which to motivate you. Most people struggle to understand how somebody else is motivated because they do it based on what motivates them."

Brad's words ring true: While my own inspiration has come from various people, none of them actually motivated me. When I was extrinsically motivated, it was based largely on what others thought about me. My inner desire to win was based on extrinsic rewards. Only I had the power to change that.

You have the power to do the same thing for yourself. Others can guide you, but only you can determine what internally motivates you. This explains why two people can walk away from a motivational seminar and one can feel highly motivated, while the other feels as if he got nothing from the hours of listening. The motivation doesn't actually come from the speaker, but from how you take in what you hear and how it resonates within you.

Applications in Life

I still enjoy success and winning, it's just that I define it differently from how I did early in my career. Success and winning now validate that I

A NEW VISION

The Irlen Institute in Southern California was founded and led by the intrinsic motivation of a former school psychologist who accidentally landed in a business.

Helen Irlen, after years of failing to understand why many students continually struggled to read despite all sorts of interventions, took it upon herself to personally figure out what was holding them back.

Leaving her school position, she worked on research studies, and, in time, discovered that the trouble many young people, as well as adults, had while trying to read was not visual but was a disconnect in the pathway from the eyes to the brain. They saw words and letters moving around on the page, much in the same way that we see an optical illusion appear to be moving on a piece of paper. What she discovered was that color could make a difference for both young and old readers, and by using colored overlays, they could read without difficulty. However, since no two people are alike, everyone seemed to need their own blend of colors.

In time, the colored overlays became colored lenses, and, thanks to an Australian journalist visiting the United States, word spread onto Australian TV about this great find. Eventually it spread to New Zealand, Great Britain, and other parts of the world, and then came back to the United States.

Pretty soon, much to her surprise, Irlen had an international business that she never planned to start. She also discovered that the same filters that helped children read could help people get rid of the headaches, migraines, light sensitivity, nausea, and other symptoms from various disorders including head injuries such as concussions. Even NHL players, and members of the military, started coming in to get fitted for the special filters to rid themselves of their symptoms from such injuries.

A NEW VISION, continued

Yet, through it all, Irlen does not talk about business but instead talks about helping children read and helping soldiers, and so many others, recapture the life they knew before their injuries. She is a marvelous example of how the intrinsic motivation to keep challenging herself to learn more and help others has become the most fulfilling part of her life.

Says Irlen, "When I get a letter from a parent whose child is reading without headaches or feeling sick or squinting under fluorescent lights, I feel so happy."

am making good progress, which is my personal goal. Failure, in turn, reminds me that there is still work to do to master whatever it is that I'm working on.

Gaining knowledge is one of the most significant personal rewards for intrinsically motivated people. Albert Einstein talked about intrinsic motivation as "the enjoyment of seeing and searching." Health, fitness, and well-being—physical and mental—are also frequently mentioned in studies as being among the most significant internal motivations. Personal satisfaction also comes from skills enhancement, along with enlightenment, understanding, reconciling, and self-discovery.

Of course motivation in life is also contextual. Someone who enjoys bicycling for the fitness, fresh air, and camaraderie of a cycling club may be asked to participate in a race for charity, where the winner gets more money for the cause. Suddenly, she is now extrinsically motivated to compete for the purpose of raising more money, an external motivation. Sometimes personal financial rewards can tip the scale. The young artist may become a graphic designer to pay the bills. Doing something because one enjoys it can easily coexist with doing the same thing out of necessity. The artist can employ her art for the joy of it, while also making a living doing it.

Each year nearly 50,000 people participate in the New York Marathon, while many others run in the Boston, Los Angeles, Disney, or other marathons. Most of these people know they will not win, will not be written about in the newspapers, will not generate a fan base from their efforts. They run for fitness and health, the fulfillment of a dream, a bucket list goal, or simply something to add to their personal history.

There are also participants who have overcome significant setbacks to run, such as a man who competed after losing his legs. Yet, many of these same people are also motivated by a paycheck during the work week, in large part because they've got to work to pay the bills.

I have also found that motivation can and does change, which might mean that you'll find yourself making an active transition, as I did, or a transition that's led more by contextual changes. For example, the young athlete who once played for the fame and fortune might become the older athlete who is determined to continue playing to stay in shape or because of a love for the game.

Workplace Motivators

In his book *Enemies of Exploration: Self-Initiated vs. Other-Initiated Learning*, John Condry suggests that you should "Choose a job you love, and you will never have to work a day in your life."

Taking the work out of work is very appealing, yet not always easy to achieve. A sense of personal pride from doing a job, taking initiative, and/or making good decisions is a means of inner satisfaction that can build intrinsic motivation. Feeling competent at a task and having autonomy, or control, combined with satisfying relationships with others at the office can also become intrinsic motivation.

As a leader, there will be times when you see your efforts paying off. It might be a sign of customer success or the completion of a new product launch. You will look around and everyone else will be busily working. You will want to high-five someone, but there's nobody around. You will feel that inner sense of success and fulfillment. That's when you smile and feel a personal sense of accomplishment that comes from being intrinsically motivated.

From a leader's perspective, building self-satisfaction in the workplace has been shown in numerous studies to result in an improved office culture and greater individual and/or team productivity. Of course, motivation and job satisfaction are highly subjective. For example, one person may feel greater satisfaction making important

A PERFECT FIT

In 2006, when Texas native Blake Mycoskie visited Argentina, he noticed numerous people throughout the country wearing slip-on canvas shoes. Liking the look of the shoes, he took to wearing them himself. It was later, in subsequent visits to Argentina and other developing nations, that Mycoskie found that many children and adults outside of the major cities were wearing no shoes at all. For Mycoskie, this was the impetus for a unique one-for-one shoe business.

A serial entrepreneur, with several successful businesses under his belt, including a laundry business and a billboard company, as well as some unsuccessful businesses, Mycoskie started a shoe company, TOMS, an abbreviation of the word "tomorrow." The concept was not to just manufacture and sell a variety of comfortable shoes, but do so with a higher purpose. Mycoskie's intrinsic motivation was for each pair purchased, he would give one pair to a child in a country where many youngsters did not have shoes.

Since the inception of the business, TOMS has given more than 10 million pairs of new shoes to children in need. As a result, TOMS can be purchased at upscale stores like Nordstrom, Neiman Marcus, and Macy's, while also being worn by poor children in 40 countries including Argentina, Guatemala, Rwanda, Haiti, and the United States.

In the same spirit, TOMS Eyewear, launched in 2011, gives away a free pair of eyeglasses with each one purchased. And to help provide jobs, TOMS has also opened a manufacturing center in Haiti. While TOMS is a for-profit business, Blake Mycoskie is fulfilling his intrinsic desire to help others.

decisions and leading projects, while another may be more comfortable in a supporting role. Personal motivation clearly differs from one person to another.

Intrinsic motivation also works in team situations, if each team member respects and understands his or her own role and the roles of others. It's about focusing on the team's efforts and not on the competition or on getting your own individual praise. If nobody needs to be the star, then everyone can give their all to the team. As legendary UCLA basketball coach John Wooden said, "It is amazing how much can be accomplished if no one cares who gets the credit."

J. K. Rowling was motivated to write the Harry Potter books because she was simply trying to create stories to read to her children. Her driving motivation was not to make billions of dollars. Some business owners start out being extrinsically motivated and make a transition in their motivational approach when they realize the love of what they do is stronger than battling to be the best. From personal experience, I must say that it is a wonderful transition and the personal rewards are much greater.

CHAPTER FIVE

YOUR PERSONAL ROAD MAP FOR SUCCESS

What would I do when my days of competing as a pro athlete ended? Would I find another job that I found purpose in? Would I even be able to find a place to apply my drive to succeed? Did I have any value to the world outside of my athletic ability?

These were some of my biggest fears during my years as an athlete. I wasn't afraid of getting injured. I wasn't afraid of failing to reach my goals. I wasn't afraid of not living up to expectations. It was what came next that worried me. I had seen teammates leave sports and move into the "real world" with little or no plan in place for their future. They often ended up struggling to find their way and some became very depressed. I wanted to do everything in my power to make sure that didn't happen in my life.

I needed a road map, or at least a map with some clear points of interest. I was determined not to find myself aimless once my playing days were over. So I dove in and began to plant seeds for a possible future career path. Most of these seeds—everything from real estate ventures to various business plans—never grew. But two seeds ended up growing into a bigger passion that I could have ever imagined, and both were created from my own personal road map.

Starting a new venture from scratch should feel like jumping out of an airplane and assembling the parachute on the way down. When I first started Integrate, a company that helps marketers automate customer generation, I had an idea of what the product would ultimately become, but it took us several product cycles and a couple of years before we found out what our business was really all about. As is most often the case, that happened largely through trial and error. That's normal; it's part of what will happen on a road map.

If your path is like most, here's how it will work:

▷ You will start out with a personal road map, and when you find your passion, you will also develop a business road map.

▷ Your journey will start at point A, but point B will not be linear; there is often no straight line between the two.

▷ You will plant seeds toward your personal goals and see which ones grow into a passion. When you find a seed that starts to grow, you will chart a course to follow that growth.

▷ Should that become a passion and a business, as was the case for me, you will then plant seeds (typically more calculated ones) within your business and see which ones work. This is the start of your business road map.

Climbing a mountain where your ultimate goal lives at the summit often involves taking two steps forward and one step back. Your road map should help you so you don't get stuck. The road map to success, for the majority of successful entrepreneurs, has several stops along the way. Some are stepping stones, while others are disappointments from which you need to recover.

Consider the story of Tony Bates, who I first met at an Olympic fundraiser. He worked directly for John Chambers, chairman of the board and CEO at Cisco. After 14 years at Cisco, he became the CEO of Skype and led the company through an $8.5 billion acquisition by Microsoft. After joining Microsoft, Tony was one of the tech company's top choices to succeed former CEO Steve Ballmer when he stepped down. When he wasn't chosen, Tony left and went on to become president of GoPro, which makes high-definition cameras, that are rugged, and lightweight. They are wearable or mountable on almost anything and are often used to capture extreme activities. Perhaps this doesn't seem unusual, as CEOs do move around. But what I love about Tony's story is that he set in writing his intention to become the CEO of Skype while he was still at Cisco. He wrote down the names of three companies that he was going to become CEO of some day, and Skype was one of them.

Of course, you don't have to be a big-time CEO to use the power of intention to get your road map ready. When I was 10 years old, I told my mom and dad that someday I was going to become an Olympian and get drafted into the NFL. I have always enjoyed setting big goals, and my parents encouraged me to do so growing up. Once I discovered my passion for business, again I set a big goal. Following this process always gives me something to direct my energy toward achieving.

No matter what, I always had a few goals in mind and left room to make a change on my road map if necessary. You may want to be a professional chef, a nurse, a surgeon, a retail store owner, or all of the above. The point is, start by defining your passions and your goals—even on paper as Tony Bates did—before creating your road map, and you'll already have the makings of a definitive plan. And don't be afraid to aim high, with big goals.

Plotting and Planning: Building in Increments

Google wasn't built in a day, and neither will you reach your primary goal in that time. A journey is the sum of the many parts. In football, there are numerous plays that need to be executed before you can reach the goal of winning the game, and numerous games to be won before you can reach the goal of winning a championship.

In business, production, marketing, sales, and other departments will have their tasks and responsibilities. Budgets will need to be created and adjusted several times over, products and services will need to be developed, sales will need to be made, and orders will need to be fulfilled before you see success. All these incremental activities are necessary to reaching a goal. You'll want to focus on the pieces of the journey as you build your road map, not just the end goal or the quickest way to get from point A to point B.

Of course, not all these incremental steps will go as planned. If I lost a major client, I would need to go back to my database and identify

POST-GAME ANALYSIS

Behind every success story is a series of incremental steps necessary to reaching that goal. Take a look at a goal you've already achieved. How did you get there? Analyzing those steps might reveal a path that can help you climb the next mountain.

To do that, on a piece of paper list:

1. Your goal

2. Steps you took to get there (training, practice, studying, getting a coach, etc.)

3. Obstacles you faced

4. How you fared

5. What you took away from that experience—what did you learn? How did it (or will it) help you in pursuit of future goals?

By reviewing goals you have reached for in the past, you can better focus on creating your personal, and later business, road map for the future.

my second biggest contact, then readjust to focus on them. It's neither the end of the world nor does it need to be a major failure. Instead, that next-biggest contact or the next thing on the horizon is where I refocus my attention; it becomes part of my new plan within the scheme of the larger goal of building and running a successful company. Each new incremental goal becomes your new mountain to climb as you travel the road to your final goal.

By nature, we tend to spend a lot of our time focused on these points in life where we look under the microscope. Sometimes we spend so much time pursuing one goal, or trying to nurture a particular seed, that we don't see others growing around us. In business, it's easy to fall into the trap of analyzing the sales numbers over and over again without looking at the bigger picture. There are plenty of stories of businesses like Kodak that are so microfocused on longtime reliable products that they are slow to see the changes in the industry that may set them behind the competition.

How many people find themselves so busy planning a meeting, event, or activity that they lose sight of the purpose of that meeting, event, or activity? I'm sure most meeting planners, or conference planners, could provide plenty of stories recounting clients that got lost in the little details.

That's why it's important to train yourself to stop, step back, look through the telescope, and focus on the really important things instead of getting bogged down by all the minutia.

The Time Is Now

Today is the youngest that you will ever be. For many people, one obstacle to creating and executing a road map is the belief that there's plenty of time to figure it all out. But the truth is, we only have a small window of time in which to create the life that was intended for us. There is no set time frame for a road map, but you do not want to drag it out too long, or you might not be poised to seize opportunities as they come up.

To avoid this, you might want to list milestones along the way. Athletes often say that if they don't reach a certain point by the age of

25 or 27 they will choose a different course. Business professionals might decide that if they don't reach a certain level in the company by age 35, they will begin looking elsewhere for new jobs. A lawyer, for example, may set age 45 as the age he expects to become a partner in the firm.

For me, sport was my first love, and I attacked my goals with every ounce of passion that I had. But I knew sports had a relatively short shelf life in relation to the average lifespan of a human being, so I also tried not to remain singularly focused—and that makes a big difference. I always kept a watchful eye out for opportunities in the periphery that could be advantageous to my long-term future. When I was 19, I was an Olympian, World Champion, the number-one ranked skier in the world, and a freshman All-American football player at the University of Colorado.

Athletically, I was on top of the world. It was a great feeling to be accomplished at such a young age, but it also scared me. I was living out my fairy tale, but I couldn't escape the thought of what my life was going to look like when athletics was over. I was scared of the possibility that the best part of my life would have already happened. You don't have to be a professional athlete to have the same concerns about what's coming up next. People constantly wonder where their careers will take them. Sure, you may love your job, have a good relationship with your colleagues, and work in a field you enjoy. But, at some point, the industry may change and your company may be hit with layoffs or shut down or move to another location. You may not write down your intent to be the next CEO of Skype, but the time is now for you to think about other goals you may have, passions you could explore. You need to take some time to plant seeds.

For me, that meant imagining a future beyond athletics, and it meant making sure I had not just one, but a few options. One of my first business ventures was in residential real estate in Colorado. It was a logical path for me, in some ways, because growing up I had watched my parents make very good property investments and earn a lot of money from the appreciation of their real estate assets. It looked like a sure thing! So I connected with some corporate leasing companies, and I would buy the units, have them professionally furnished, and then turn them over to a corporate leasing company who would fully manage

STOPS ALONG THE WAY

I made several stops in my effort to plot a course for my post-athletic future. Among them:

▷ I created The Professional Athletes Education Initiative. It was an initiative aimed to link all major professional leagues with Ivy League schools that would provide players with the ability to enroll in classes and programs in their off-seasons. I thought it would be a great way to connect athletes from different sports in an academic environment that could stimulate their planning for their life after sports. The initiative never got off the ground, but it was a meaningful exercise.

▷ I did broadcasting of sporting events, a path some athletes have found really successful after their on-field careers.

▷ I got into entertainment broadcasting, hosting a show at the MTV beach house, then manning the red carpet for "E!" and later serving as the host of *OnDemand* for Starz Networks, interviewing musicians like The Fray, James Blunt, and Train.

They were all stops on the road for me, yet I didn't find my calling in any of them, nor did I see them as long-term endeavors.

the listing while I was off competing. The goal was to have the renters pay off my mortgage and eventually sell the properties for a profit. In theory, that's how it was supposed to work. However at the time the real estate market tanked and it did not work out as I had imagined.

In Search of Your Passion

Sometimes you might feel lost along the road. At age 27, I was entirely unsure of what to do next. I needed some inspiration and direction. So,

I enrolled in a program at University of Pennsylvania's Wharton School of Business focused on finance entrepreneurship.

START HERE, NOT HERE

It's important that you know where to start your trip and who is going to finance it. Three things I learned when coming out of the Wharton program were:

1. Never invest in a nightclub.

2. Never invest in a restaurant.

3. Lose somebody else's money before you lose your own.

Wharton professor Peter Linnemen, who became a friend and mentor, taught me the third point, and it stuck with me. One of the blind spots for pro athletes who are transitioning into the real world is a belief that they can do anything. This attitude is paramount in sports when you're competing with the world's best athletes. But it doesn't carry over into the real world. As a result, many former athletes jump into businesses in which they have no experience.

This is one reason why so many former pro athletes end up bankrupt. The truth is that athletes, along with most of us, need to get involved in an industry before diving in headfirst. So many athletes start businesses and lose a fortune rather than first taking a position in the industry or being a minor partner and learning all about how the business works.

It's not just athletes. We all must learn an industry prior to seriously investing in it. Once I learned about marketing and got exposure to it, I checked off that box on my own road map. The knowledge I gained about marketers' pain points led me to starting Integrate to create a solution. New ideas and new businesses often come from examining problems or pain points that you or others have and providing the solutions for those problems.

Taking classes is a great way to discover where your passions lie. Many colleges and universities offer short intensive courses or part-time classes that meet weekly. There are also numerous online courses that can cost as little as a few hundred dollars per semester. These can be a great way to test out something you think you might be passionate about. Coursera.org, for example, has nearly 900 courses available from some of the finest universities in the world, including Princeton and Stanford. By exploring opportunities and reading about other areas of interest, you can discover what direction you want to take.

For me, I knew I was interested in entrepreneurship, but knew little about it. Once I began learning about internet businesses and how they worked, I was hooked. My interest in starting an internet business grew quickly and I became even more obsessed about starting such a company than I was about playing football. Now, instead of studying a playbook at 2 o'clock in the morning, I was up putting together a business plan. There was a natural evolution in my life toward this direction and I was enthusiastically learning as much as I could about it.

Your road map will begin by planting seeds and continue as those seeds lead you to try various possibilities. Very rarely is anything love at first sight, whether that means meeting your spouse, buying a house, or finding a career you are passionate about. There will be some starts and stops, but it's important that you keep searching for something you feel passionate about. Once you do, learn about it and invest your mental and emotional energy. Don't be afraid to give it 100 percent.

For most people, changing careers can be very scary, especially if you have a family who is depending on you. One of my coaches in college, Chris Wilson, used to always tell me: "Jeremy, never allow fear to get in your way of making your dreams come true." His advice was timely: I was a 175-pound freshman football player staring at linebackers that were twice my size. But his advice has also translated to many areas of my life outside of athletics.

Once you have set an intention and a goal, don't just dream about it, attack it.

Passion + Need = Business Opportunity

Following Wharton Professor Peter Linnemen's advice, I decided not to lose my capital by starting a business I did not know much about. Instead, I went into business with a friend who funded the creation of MDinfo, Inc. It was there, as head of customer acquisition, that I learned a lot about recognizing pain points in the business. Working in this company gave me the opportunity to learn about marketing, about

SETTING GOALS FOR YOURSELF—AND ONLY YOURSELF

Katherine Keller, president of Chumcubo Designs, an online marketing and graphic design agency, isn't just focused on her own business. She also spends time helping small entrepreneurs point themselves in the right direction, preparing people for the ups and downs of business that she's been through plenty of times.

As Keller states in her article "The Answers to These 3 Questions Will Get You Through the Low Points" for Entrepreneur.com, "Entrepreneurial life creates the highest of highs and the lowest of lows. It is a journey of never-ending emotions. The true leaders emerge when times are tough, gut-wrenching decisions are called for and mistakes are made."

Keller finds it easier to bounce back from the lows that came along with following her own goals and passions. That is, if you are a people pleaser, you aren't pleasing yourself and you're more likely to drown your own entrepreneurial dreams.

"It is said that when people pleasers die, they see the life of someone else flash before their eyes," she says. "Is there anything more somber than to put forth all of the blood, sweat and tears into your life only to come to the end of your journey and realize that you've been dead inside all along?"

the online world, and to really understand what the industry was about before committing to my own business.

The goal of MDinfo, which has since gone out of business, was to build a global social network of doctors, nurses, and healthcare professionals to share their knowledge in a personal way with consumers. WebMD had captured most of the market share in the healthcare content category, but we believed that there was a need for a way for people to have a more intimate experience with a healthcare expert on the web. We wanted to build a cadre of experts to help people—helping those experts build their own brands in the process. It was a traditional marketplace business, but those can be the hardest to succeed in. If there's an imbalance of supply or demand, the user experience can be awful and customers flee.

It was challenging to get healthcare experts to contribute content for the benefit of building their brand and helping people. But we learned that there were about 10,000 questions on MDinfo that covered what 90 percent of people would ask. So we built an algorithm that identified these questions (namely around acne, diabetes, and sexual issues) and served consumers repeat answers by the doctors and nurses. Readers could vote on whether each answer was helpful or not. Soon we had hundreds of doctors, nurses, and healthcare experts contributing content to our most popular threads.

At our peak, MDinfo captured more than 90 million unique visitors from more than 36 countries in one month. We didn't sell display ads because very few healthcare advertisers want their ads to appear next to user-generated content that they have no control over. Instead, we monetized lead generation. When a consumer asked a question in a specific healthcare category, they could opt for different deals and products in that category.

The business ultimately brought in about $250,000 per month. That's when we took the next step on our path to success. We got into the world of clinical trial patient recruitment, which is one of the biggest challenges for every major pharmaceutical company. It's not easy to find people who want to participate in a clinical trial, but it's essential that pharmaceutical companies find these individuals. Every

CURVEBALLS: WHEN ALL DOES NOT GO AS PLANNED

Every new business has a projected revenue chart, and 100 percent of the time it is up and to the right. But the reality is, very few companies ever experience that type of unimpeded growth. Growing a business is like climbing a mountain. It's very easy to draw a straight line on a map from base camp to the summit, but the reality is that you will encounter all kinds of detours, obstacles, and barriers along the way. The key to getting to the top is simpler than you might think—and it's also a bit counterintuitive. It's knowing ahead of time that you will not have a clear, unencumbered path ahead of you.

In my years at Integrate, we've hired good people, but also had some not-so-good ones along the way. I've made business decisions that have proven to be fruitful, but also had some disasters in the process of growing the company. The point is, on the road to success you will encounter all sorts of obstacles and you need to be flexible when they rear their ugly heads. You need to be prepared to slay a few dragons along the way.

Remember, success isn't linear . . . there is no straight line to follow. Some businesses have had to make major pivots and take a totally new direction before they've reached success.

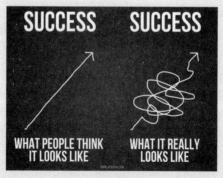

Reprinted with the permission of Semih Akalin, Atbreak.com.

day that a new clinical trial is delayed due to the lack of participants, it can cost the pharmaceutical company millions of dollars.

Although clinical trial patient recruitment is lucrative, it's also very difficult to target the right people. For example, we once had to find people over the age of 55, with a body mass index over 30, taking Lexapro, living in ZIP codes 94105 to 94110, and having the adverse effect of dry skin. Yes, a marketer's nightmare. But if successful, we could be paid $50,000 per person we found. Scaling patient recruitment for clinical trials was a significant challenge.

But here's where having a personal success goal and a flexible road map to that goal helped immensely. This biggest pain point that I encountered at MDinfo led to the creation of Integrate. As head of customer acquisition, I became very frustrated with the inefficiencies within the marketing department as it tried to bring in new customers. At a high level, all our systems were disconnected and none of our marketing software meaningfully connected to the others. I had to hire numerous people to manually pull data to and from various systems and use an Excel spreadsheet to try and make sense of it all. And the problem got bigger and more costly as the company grew.

DISTANCE YOURSELF FROM PREVIOUS JOURNEYS

In athletics I was forced to teach myself how to have a short memory. If you allow the mistakes of the past to affect you mentally, they will compound and can materialize into a downward spiral. Your opinion of yourself and your new road map to success should not be predicated, or clouded, by previous ones. You only want to take your learning experiences with you. Whether I was at the World Cup skiing championships, the Olympics, or making a big deal in business, if I carried past failures or disappointment with me, it would show in my eyes and my attitude. When this happens, you can lose your swagger and confidence.

I couldn't find a product on the market that integrated data, so we decided to build one. If it worked, we could potentially save MDinfo more than $350,000 per month, while increasing engagement rates on the site by 30 percent. And it did work.

We realized that if this solved the primary pain point of our marketing department, the software might be able to do the same for other businesses. It was this discovery that set up the next steps in my entrepreneurial life and on my road map . . . Integrate!

Making Pivots

Startups have to be nimble and open to change, especially in the first few years. Groupon started off as an online collective action and fundraising platform before pivoting into the social commerce space. There's a fine balance between retaining products that fit your market and stubbornly trying to hold onto ideas, products, or marketing strategies that are not attracting a significant target market. Sometimes you can pound a market, but the product is just not working. It's the old square pegs into round holes theory, and, of course, that does not work.

There are many stories of major pivots in well-known businesses. A few examples:

▷ Flickr was a role-playing gaming site for a couple years before emerging as the popular photo-sharing social media site.

▷ Apple started out selling computer kits to kids before making their own computers and emerging as a $700 billion business.

▷ Lego started by making wooden ducks. A few years after a fire burned down the factory, management decided to switch to plastic toys, and what emerged? The interlocking bricks that have spawned a multibillion-dollar business that encompasses TV shows, movies, creation contests, and more.

▷ Nokia began as a paper mill and expanded into making rubber goods before moving to electronics and eventually to mobile phones.

▷ Avon was started by a door-to-door book salesman who gave away free samples of perfume. The perfume got better reviews than the books, so he did a complete pivot and dumped the books in favor of starting the California Perfume Company, a precursor of Avon.

CASE STUDY: PIVOTING TO SUCCESS

Another great story of change, or pivoting, comes from Eric Roza. After a number of years in various businesses, Eric, a friend of mine, in January 2007 joined a company called NextAction. At the time, the company helped small retail businesses target their catalogs to the intended shoppers. It was based on predictive analytics, which meant bringing together a lot of data and then building statistical models to figure out the likelihood of a customer being interested in a catalog from a given retailer.

"In 2007 and 2008, if your only business was targeting print catalogs you knew you had problems since the catalog market was not exactly growing," Eric explained to me. The company took a major hit soon after when the United States Postal Service levied what was roughly a 40 percent increase in the cost of postage for catalogs.

"We were now relying entirely on print catalogs in a digital world with increasing postage. Before we knew it, the business was literally plummeting into oblivion," Eric recounted. He was second in command at the company at the time, and was later asked to be CEO. "We were declining by 40 percent a year and we didn't know where the bottom was. My first action as CEO was to cut my own salary by 20 percent along with the salaries of the other 110 employees, which was far better than layoffs," Eric told me. He says he wouldn't have accepted the helm if he hadn't already been an executive at the company.

PIVOTING TO SUCCESS, continued

It was also around this time that the company started building and investing in an online model. That idea came from the belief that the kind of data being gathered—information about what people had purchased in the past—was the kind of data that would be valuable online. The concept was to provide such information to advertisers who would want to focus on what people had actually purchased before, rather than focusing on what they were reading about or what they were saying they would purchase.

For a year the business struggled, defaulting on its bank covenants and finding no sympathy with existing investors who no longer wanted to put any more money into the company. Eric describes the situation as having been "quite tense, especially with the board of directors."

"This was a company that was very successful in the past on a small scale, so expectations had been set high," recalls Eric. "But the company was now worth almost nothing by late 2008." He knew he had to raise money at any cost, take it on the chin, and figure out how much or how little the company was worth. That's a tough spot to be in. "At the end of the day, we needed to generate new capital and we needed to have a board [of directors] that believed in the vision that I had for the company. If they did not believe in what we were trying to do, I knew the situation was futile."

Roza reached out to General Catalyst, a leading venture capital firm, whose executive-in-residence, Rob Gierkink, and founder, David Fialkow, agreed to fund the company's digital future. NextAction was rebranded as Datalogix in October of 2009—and became one of the most significant companies in the world of digital advertising. With its aggregated data about customer purchasing from 1,500 sources, the company successfully went after major online clients such as Facebook, Google, Twitter, and Yahoo!.

PIVOTING TO SUCCESS, continued

And that proved to be a turning point—a new direction on the road map. "Our data had to be everywhere so it could benefit advertisers," explained Eric. "If a big consumer brand like Kraft or Chrysler decided to advertise, they wouldn't know if the ads were driving the product or not, because 94 percent of the sales are offline—so we became the guys who connected the dots for the big advertisers and big digital publishers." Datalogix became the link between the advertising and what customers were buying in stores or at car dealers.

And guess what? Eric's plan worked. He led a major pivot and took a company from the brink of disaster, in a new "digital" direction. Today, Datalogix—recently bought out by Oracle for $1.2 billion—works with 80 of the top 100 brands in America and is a leader in its field. Ironically, thanks to its infusion of new data and hiring of dozens of the country's best data scientists, even the company's legacy catalog business experienced a renaissance and continues to grow. Overall, the company has grown 500 percent in five years. By late 2014, the Colorado-based company had nearly 450 employees and had raised more than $90 million in funding, far more than the company was worth when it hit bottom in 2008.

My Personal Road Map

My entry into tech happened in 2009 when I decided to attend a TEDMED conference in San Diego, California. I had heard great things about the event, an annual conference focusing on health and medicine, and because I am so passionate about health, I thought it would be a good place for me to learn more.

The first night I attended the opening dinner, and I did not know a single person there. A cool-looking guy with long blond hair sat next to me and we started chatting. It turned out that he was a big Philadelphia Eagles fan, so we had a lot to discuss. I asked him what he did, and he told me he worked at YouTube. Somewhere between dinner and dessert I overheard him telling someone else that he didn't just work there, he had co-founded YouTube. Chad Hurley is one of the smartest and most humble guys that I've met in tech. We hung out the whole conference, and today he is one of my good friends. He is also the one who introduced me to two other good friends: Google's managing partner Bill Maris and Google's co-founder Sergey Brin.

When I started my own company, I thought that it would be nice to not have a boss. I was used to operating in that type of environment from my skiing days, where I called the shots. However, what I discovered is that I actually have many bosses. They are Integrate's customers—and they are far more demanding than any direct boss that I could have. However, I think the most important metric to every business is customer success. I'm not focused on an exit or IPO; I focus every day on how, as an entire company, we can help to make our customers more successful.

I am also very passionate about building a great culture because life is too short not to love what you do and the people you work with. I feel lucky to have found something that drives me to succeed as much as athletics did so quickly after retiring from sports—and that is a bigger blessing than any of the medals that I won.

Although a little broad, here is a general step-by-step list of how to get where you are going that has worked well for me.

1. Plant seeds and constantly observe your garden, looking for growth opportunities and pockets of passion.
2. Network.
3. Set an intention and write it down, like Tony Bates did.
4. Network.
5. Learn the business thoroughly through classes, internships, seminars, books, networking, etc.
6. Network.
7. Work for someone else first, and keep learning.
8. Network.

9. Conduct due diligence on product market fit—prior to writing a business plan.
10. Network.
11. Find talent, steal talent, and keep talent happy.
12. Network.
13. Talk to your customers consistently to capture feedback.
14. Network.

And don't forget, always be flexible. There is no straight line from point A to point B. Success is never linear.

CHAPTER SIX

REDEFINE YOURSELF:
YOUR NEW DESTINY

The toughest part about starting off in a new career is the fear of the unknown. You are suddenly the newcomer, like a new kid at school all over again, wondering how things are going to play out. For me, the toughest part of redefining myself as an entrepreneur was that it was all new to me and I didn't know if I would be any good at it.

One of the biggest reasons professional athletes go broke after their playing days are over: They make foolish investments. Wharton professor Peter Linneman's advice to me, to lose someone else's money before risking my own, wasn't just good sense, it was a road map. The advice was meant to encourage me to join a company first, learn the ropes and then create a startup with my own capital.

A New Challenge

When I left athletics, I wanted to completely redefine myself. I wanted to climb a mountain that was entirely new to me. Whether you have enjoyed great success or a thousand mediocre or failed endeavors, when you try something new, you are stepping into a different arena, with different rules, different players, and different unforeseen challenges. People in the new space might already know you, as was my case. But even so, those connections knew me as an athlete. I didn't know how they would react to me now as an entrepreneur. Would they see me as a fish out of water? Would they embrace my ideas?

One of the biggest challenges when embarking on a new career is controlling your own psychology. Essentially, you have to be mentally comfortable feeling, well, a little uncomfortable. Chances are, you've spent a great amount of time in your life working toward, and maybe reaching, a goal. It is understandable that you will be uncomfortable starting again; transitions are scary, but they are also the moments when you feel the most alive. When Steve Jobs was fired from Apple, it was a very mentally challenging experience, but he recounted it as a time in his life when he felt most alive.

For me, after dedicating so much of my life to football and skiing, I was excited to start over, at the bottom of a new and exciting mountain.

Apolo Ohno, a good friend of mine, is best known for his eight Olympic speed skating medals (two gold, two silver, and four bronze) at three separate winter Olympic Games—not to mention his 21 medals at the World Championships. But he's also in the midst of making a post-sports transition. He knows that apprehension that many of us feel all too well.

"Making such a transition for an athlete is never easy, it doesn't matter how much money you amassed or how successful you were," Apolo tells me. "When you've spent your entire life focused solely on one thing, it's hard to refocus. The transition is usually painful and difficult for an athlete."

As an athlete, whose goal is often to become the best at the one thing you do, "your career path in life is magnified and you usually

COMING FULL CIRCLE

When she was in college, Gail Sagel's father asked her what she planned to do for a career. She explained that with people living longer, she saw a need for an anti-aging approach to skin care and makeup. Her father looked at her, shook his head, and told her she should go to law school or business school. She dutifully followed her father's advice and went on to work on Wall Street after graduating from the University of Maryland School of Business, double majoring in economics and marketing.

During college, Gail interned with First Options of Chicago, where she learned how to trade options on the floor of the American Stock exchange. Soon, she was working for Bear Stearns in the United States and abroad. While working with clients in Paris, France, she would spend her downtime visiting spas and observing cosmetic trends at the makeup counters of Le Bon Marche and the Galeries Lafayette. For Gail, these excursions were a much-needed break from the many hours spent in a cutthroat trading environment with a cast of characters that she likened to those in the movie *The Wolf of Wall Street*, and at the time, in the late 1980s, most of her colleagues were male. In 1993, after Gail gave birth to twins, she resigned after struggling to find good child-care options.

Five years later, with her children entering grade school and her marriage over, Gail, now living in Connecticut, needed to return to work. The culture of the financial industry had changed since she'd been out of it, and so had the finance opportunities in Connecticut, where many hedge funds had set up shop. Gail was able to find work at a small Connecticut firm. Yet she was still doing something she didn't feel passionate about. Then one day, while biking home from work, she was hit by a car.

COMING FULL CIRCLE, continued

In the ambulance, Gail recalls thinking the accident was a sign that she needed to change her life. Following a full recovery, Gail was reminded, by her best college girlfriend, of her long-time passion for makeup and just how good she had been at performing makeovers. In 1999, she opened FACES Beautiful, starting in her living room and developing into a luxury makeup studio, upscale salon, and beauty boutique in Connecticut. Gail had come full circle from her earliest passions all the way back to what she loved to do. She had been very successful in the financial world. She had not failed, but the environment in that industry had failed her.

Sometimes, failure isn't from the efforts of the individual but from a toxic environment from which you need to escape. Now, more than 15 years later, the studio continues to be successful and Gail has created a makeup and a skincare brand which are sold nationally online.

Passion can be found at any age—and rediscovered if you left it behind.

don't have time to do anything else," Apolo told me—and I can relate. "Some people find the time to go to school, but for the most part, at that level of commitment, you simply cannot afford to diversify your life very much." For athletes, making change is even harder because the level of adrenaline in athletics, especially at the peak level, is high, and "we're constantly searching for the same kind of stimuli."

That's definitely not easy, as both Apolo and I—and countless others—have found.

It's never easy to find the time, whether in sports or in business, to find a new venture to explore, much less gain some knowledge and experience in that area of interest. For someone who's spent years in the fast-paced, competitive world of finance, it can be quite eye-opening to suddenly find yourself slowly trying to build a business as a new entrepreneur.

Taking Something with You

For anyone changing careers, it's easier to move to something new when you realize you can take something with you from your first act.

In his career transition, for instance, Apolo says he learned "to apply aspects of sports, such as how to train and how I represented myself during the Olympic games. My goal was to take those same attributes and apply them toward business opportunities, whether it was in broadcasting, the tech industry, natural resources, supplements and neutriceuticals, clothing, or brokering deals."

Apolo says he tried to find a similar path as he did when he was skating and apply the same sort of focus and competitive training-oriented mindset to whatever came next. "Of course I realized that it was not going to be as instantaneous as my sport, where a race lasted 40 seconds, but I'm always looking to improve and to see where I can go from here," he says. "That's what drives me."

Keys to Changing Careers

Whether you are walking away from a business that didn't work out, a dream that did not come true, or a successful career where you accomplished your goals, I think it's a good idea to dedicate some time to exploring other ideas. One of them could eventually lead you to the next chapter of your professional career. Even during my dual athletic career, when almost every second of my day was allocated to training or competing, I would find time to explore future possibilities and ideas.

Besides finding something that you enjoy, take the time to research your new area of interest and understand the current market. Many successful business owners put a lot of time into staying current on their industry and reading everything they can to understand the space and learn about the competition. This type of research should start before you jump into your new business venture.

When starting Integrate, we needed to know whether we were entering a growing market or a saturated one. We needed to know if there was a market for our product, how big that market was (and the growth potential), and whether we had significant competition. Reading and studying then, and now, was and is vital to our success. You may be passionate about starting a specific type of business, but, based on your due diligence, the timing might not be right. If that's the case, you will either need to be patient, modify your product or idea, or explore some of the other seeds you have planted.

NETWORKING THROUGH LINKEDIN

A great place for networking is in the social media—and particularly LinkedIn. The thing that I use LinkedIn the most for now is finding talented people who might be interested in joining Integrate. It is easy to search by company name, job title, and level of experience.

A few other ways to utilize the site:

▷ The advanced feature on top of your profile page shows the connections of your connections by category—you can then ask your connections if they are okay with you reaching out to their connections.

▷ Join groups in your area of business and join the conversation or start a thread with a thought-provoking question; respond privately with people you think you'd like to add to your network.

▷ Stay current. Update your profile page, share current news, and update and link to your own blog often. If you have a premium account you can also use Open Link to send messages to people to whom you are not yet connected.

▷ Read what your connections are sharing and responding to. Let people know you are paying attention to their news and information.

▷ It's also important to open doors and grab people's attention. Give them something unique or provocative (yet professional).

Once you've found your way, you can't stop studying. Proven entrepreneurs, like Tony Bates of GoPro, continue monitoring their industry every single day.

It's also important to expand your network from the start. It can be intimidating at first, trying to connect with people you might not know. But social media—especially LinkedIn—has made reaching out to new business contacts easier than ever. LinkedIn is a great tool to connect with people who can be a resource for you when you start looking into a new idea. You might be surprised to find that you already have more contacts than you think.

Along with meeting people on LinkedIn through groups or mutual connections, I also find it fascinating and inspirational to talk with people who are way ahead of me, with years of experience. Provided they have the time, people who have "been there and done that" are often willing to share a lot of their wisdom with you. Some of those people, whose opinions and suggestions I regard very highly, have become advisors and mentors of mine in life, work, and this book.

Successful Transitions

In 2012, I was asked by Young Presidents Organization, a global network of young chief executives, to give a keynote talk at their annual ski trip to Squaw Valley, California. David Karnstedt was one of the first people that I met there. He had recently sold his software advertising company, Efficient Frontier, to Adobe for $400 million, and because we were both building companies in a similar space, we had a lot to talk about. Today, David serves on Integrate's board of advisors and is someone for whom I have a tremendous amount of respect.

Among the most inspiring things about David: He discovered a passion in a career he hated and transformed it into an industry that he enjoyed.

"I sold surgical equipment once upon a time, working from my home," he says. "My office was essentially every hospital in the Midwest. I hated that job. I didn't fail at it—in fact, I won rookie of the year at a sales conference. Then I quit," says David, who wasn't happy in surgical sales. However, there was something about the work that he did love. He was in medical sales at the time when arthroscopic and endoscopic surgery were becoming popular, and David discovered he had a real passion for the technology involved. "I loved this stuff. I just needed to find a job in another industry," explains David, and he did just that. He later went on to run North American sales for Yahoo! and become the CEO of a unified software advertising platform called Efficient Frontier, a company that would later sell to Adobe for $400 million.

Finding a passion makes transitioning into a new career infinitely more interesting. For athletes and some others, the need for a second passion is so important because a career can be so fleeting.

ROGER STAUBACH'S DUAL SUCCESS STORY

If you remember watching Roger Staubach play quarterback for Navy or in the NFL for the Dallas Cowboys, I envy you. I never saw Staubach play, but I know that he was a Heisman Trophy winner in 1963, then served in the Navy in Vietnam, returning to have an 11-year career with the Dallas Cowboys, taking them to four Super Bowls and winning two of them. Staubach won a most valuable player award and made the Pro Bowl six times in the 1970s.

He is also someone I greatly admire because he transitioned from being a Hall-of-Fame quarterback to building an amazing career in real estate. Perhaps the most interesting aspect of Staubach's transition is that unlike so many athletes, myself included, he did not wait until after football to plant seeds in hopes of finding something to do. Instead, he planted them, learned a business, and immersed himself in it *while* playing football.

"When I came out of the Naval Academy in 1965, I had a four-year obligation to the service, and we had three children that were born while in the Navy. In those days, they didn't pay quarterbacks what they do

ROGER STAUBACH'S DUAL SUCCESS STORY, continued

today, and as a 27-year-old rookie with a wife and three children, I was thinking that if I got hurt and couldn't play I would need to have something else I could fall back on," Staubach recounts. "So, in the off-season I interviewed with a couple of companies and went to work for a Texas real estate firm that was going to pay me on commission. This was a good deal because I could only work there half of the year, but if I were productive I would get rewarded. What was also good was that I could learn about the real estate industry while I was still playing." Staubach worked for, and learned from, Henry S. Miller, who mentored him at what was the largest independent commercial real estate firm in the state.

According to Staubach, there were many things that he could transfer from sports into business. Among them: teamwork, perseverance, and hard work. He has said, "It takes a lot of unspectacular preparation to have spectacular results in both business and football."

Staubach says real estate was a good career move in part because he also enjoyed the competitive side of the business. In a short time, it became a passion. "It's a very competitive industry, and that was something I liked about real estate. That made it challenging and interesting for me," says Staubach, who in 1979 teamed with broker Robert Holloway to form the Holloway-Staubach Corporation. Yes, that was two years before he retired from the NFL and only a few months before he led the Cowboys to victory in Super Bowl XII over the Denver Broncos.

"After 11 seasons, I had six concussions where I was totally knocked out and I was 38 years old. I was actually coming off a really good season, and our general manager, Tex Schramm, wanted me to play two more years. In fact, he offered me one of the biggest contracts ever at that time,"

ROGER STAUBACH'S DUAL
SUCCESS STORY, continued

recalls Staubach. But his doctor had other ideas. "He told me that I'd had too many [concussions] and the next one could be serious. So, I decided to pursue my life after football and retired from the game to take on the challenge of building my company."

The lessons he took from sports served him well in his new career in business. "Like sports, you have to have the right people in the right places and they have to work well together," he says. "I worked hard at bringing in a lot of good people. I devoted enough time and energy to the real estate business so that people knew I was committed to it. They knew I wasn't just an athlete putting my name on the door."

In time, Staubach bought out Holloway and the company expanded from a Texas real estate firm into a major national real estate company, winning many major contracts globally.

In 2008, the Staubach Company was sold to Jones Lang LaSalle for $613 million. Staubach currently serves as executive chairman of Jones Lang LaSalle. He is considered by many to be the most successful superstar athlete turned entrepreneur. He also truly epitomizes the concept of planting seeds, starting out under someone else before investing your own money, and following your passions.

I love Roger Staubach's story of success. He was prescriptive about learning a new skill while he was still playing professional athletics, and like Wharton professor Peter Linnemen suggests, he worked for a real estate firm first before starting his own business. In an era where athletes are making more money than in the days of Roger Staubach, we have the opportunity to test the waters a little more carefully.

Yet, that can also backfire, as many former athletes expect many doors to open after sports simply because of their name and their previous success. They sometimes face a rude awakening when that does not happen. At the Olympic level, and even for successful athletes coming out of the NCAA, there is a time when you are not sure what comes next in life. It's easy to get immersed in sports, from the dedication and the excitement that comes with it, but hard to see what will come next.

CHAPTER SEVEN

MANAGEMENT, TEAM BUILDING, AND VICTIMS

I remember during my time with the Philadelphia Eagles how fearful players were of being cut. There was this idea that fear would build greater strength and unity. Instead, it seemed to do the opposite.

The locker room of the Pittsburgh Steelers was home to a very different feeling. Instead of fear, there was a locked-arms culture and a sense of unity.

When I left football, I recalled the difference in the management styles of these two successful NFL franchises. I didn't know it at the time, but these contrasting examples would help me formulate my own management style in years to come.

Managing Your Team: Top-Down or Bottom-Up?

Top-down management, as the name might imply, means that everything in business or sports starts at the top and works its way down to the next level of managers, or coaches, and then down to the team. While this style has been effective in some industries, utilizing a single vision and pushing it downward through the ranks can also alienate people on your team who don't feel they have a say in how things get done. Top-down can also lead to a lack of motivation among employees because they don't feel enough ownership or input in their work and the goals of the company, which usually reduces productivity.

One reason that the bottom-up approach to management is growing in popularity is because people naturally like to feel that their opinions are heard and valued. In such environments, team members feel more connected to the company's mission and empowered to help influence outcomes rather than blame management for the inefficiencies inside the business.

I experienced both styles of management in the NFL. I was a member of two very differently managed teams. My first experience came from my time with the Philadelphia Eagles, under head coach Andy Reid. He is a phenomenal, highly committed, and very knowledgeable coach. He coached the Eagles for 14 years, and more recently took a struggling Kansas City Chiefs from last place to a playoff berth in the 2013 season.

With the Eagles, a strict top-down management style ruled with fear-based motivation. In team meetings and player position meetings, you'd hear coaches, almost on a daily basis, say things like, "If you don't do XYZ, you're out of here. We'll find somebody to replace you, there are plenty of other players out there." Coaches would talk fear into the players, in hopes of motivating them.

But what happened, from my perspective, was that this type of motivation created a disconnected culture. Inside the locker room, it felt like a lot of players were on their own islands, looking over their shoulder, wondering if they would be the next one to get cut. As a result, players were looking out for themselves. As a team, it hurt our ability to build connectivity. And even though the Eagles roster of players arguably held more talent than the roster I was later on with the Pittsburgh Steelers, the Eagles never won a Super Bowl.

My other experience, with the Steelers, was completely different. The Rooney family has owned the team for decades, and it's a family-oriented organization where everyone is afforded a high level of respect. Mike Tomlin, at the time in his second year as head coach, fit this family mentality and led a bottom-up management style very well. He was the best leader that I have ever been around. His ability to unify a group of men who came from different economic, religious, and racial backgrounds, and with all kinds of individual personality quirks and strengths, was something that I had never seen before. Coach Tomlin made you feel that you were part of the Steelers family. He is firm, honest, and, at times, brutally transparent. It was a locked-arms culture and as connected of a locker room as I have ever seen. Coach Tomlin allowed you to fail, as long as you failed fast and quickly corrected it. This was in 2008, the year the Pittsburgh Steelers won their record-setting sixth Super Bowl championship in eight appearances.

I think a big reason for the Steelers' success has been due to the type of management, leadership, and motivation that are all key ingredients to building a great culture. There was a significant difference in the two environments that I played in and experienced during my time in the NFL. And I believe wholeheartedly that it impacted the final results.

As a founder and CEO, I try to follow the Steelers' way of management—fully transparent, bottom-up, and respectful of all involved. I know I appreciated working in that environment, and people who are built in our cultural mold appreciate it, too. While Andy Reid has had a successful career that will likely land him in the NFL Hall of Fame one day, what I took away from Mike Tomlin's style has worked for me in business.

The Keys to Building a Strong Team

No matter what positions you need to fill, you want to build a team of future leaders. Laszlo Bock, senior vice president of people operations

FINDING A PARTNER:
THE ART OF CO-FOUNDING

Another way to move in a new direction is by joining forces with someone else. The truth is, businesses are never the work of just one person. Behind all notable business success stories is a partner of some kind, whether or not that person shares the spotlight, takes the credit, or addresses the media. I think the biggest mistake first-time founders make, which is also quite common, is to choose a best friend as a co-founder or business partner, without considering whether or not that friend possesses a complementary skill set.

My co-founder at Integrate, who has since moved on to other ventures, complemented my blind spots well. His skill set was building technology quickly and efficiently, while mine was in leadership, business development, and sales. Sometimes you'll figure out what you lack early on and seek out people with the talents and skills you need. That's the ideal, of course. But more often in a new business, one partner tries to take on responsibilities they really don't have the skills to handle. And that rarely works out.

It's a good idea to ensure that you know what each founder brings to the table in advance and sort out what needs to be done to compensate for any shortcomings either of you might have. For example, if your partner is introverted and does not handle social situations very well, you will need to either assume more of the social role or discuss ways to make it easier for the two of you as a team to handle social situations.

Of course, it's more than just personality attributes and technical or tactical skills that you need to identify and make fit with co-founders or partners, it's also an unyielding belief in the business, its goals, and, generally, how to achieve them. You need to be aligned and ready to go to bat for each other. It's not that there won't be bumps in the relationship, but your

FINDING A PARTNER:
THE ART OF CO-FOUNDING, continued

partnership will last longer if you have a similar outlook on how things should be done. With that in mind, it's best to enter a business partnership with someone you know (or get to know) reasonably well. The business environment will throw plenty of challenges in your direction, so it's a good idea to have a similar plan for handling them.

Finally, it's crucial to develop a conflict resolution plan. That might sound silly—especially after you've found a partner with complementary skills and personality traits. Why do you need a conflict resolution plan? Because conflict happens and you cannot let it derail your partnership and your business. Of course, if you bring every issue you have a disagreement over to the table, you're going to kill the cadence and productivity.

The first couple of years my co-founder and I had a difficult time figuring out how to have healthy conflicts. We went through one period of conflict that was so bad that we didn't talk to each other for months at a time. I hated it, and it created major challenges in our business. What we worked out after a lot of trial and error was a rating system of discomfort. If either of us felt strongly about something, we would say, "I think this is a bad idea because XYZ, and it's a ten out of ten feeling of discomfort." We agreed that when one of us felt so strongly about something, we would accept that person's point of view and move on. It didn't always work, but it greatly helped us improve our ability to efficiently get past times of disagreement.

The key is to look for the yellow flags and set aside some time to talk about potential issues before they become red flags. In situations where your approach to business is fundamentally different, which my partner and I had at times, you will need to address the situation. If you try working around yellow flags for too long they will likely become red flags.

FINDING A PARTNER:
THE ART OF CO-FOUNDING, continued

Compromise is very important, but even when you do compromise, not every partnership can or will work out. Too many potential red flags early on in the process might mean that this partnership is ill-advised, so keep your eyes open for those hints, which could be as simple as X or more complex, like X, Y, and Z.

(essentially, HR) at Google, is someone for whom I have a lot of respect. Bock says it's important to look for leadership qualities from the start. This doesn't mean choosing only the former presidents of the chess club or the Boy or Girl Scouts, but instead someone who can, when necessary, step in and lead. These people with the ability to "take charge" when necessary are valued most in a leadership culture.

But as Bock emphasizes, strong team members also need to step back and relinquish power when necessary. Bock says it's important to hire people who are strong-minded and vigorously support their positions, "arguing like hell when necessary." But these same people ought to be able to, when provided with new information, step back and say, "Okay, you're right." As Bock puts it, "You need a big ego and small ego in the same person at the same time."

Such people are hard to find. In sports, or business, these are the people you can give the ball to time after time, but when the defense or business strategies change, they can accept that someone else may need to carry the ball for a while. Unselfish leaders are the ultimate hire when building a strong team.

Other characteristics that I believe are key to building a strong team in business:

1. *A good cultural fit.* I'll take a good culture fit over someone who is highly competent but a culture risk. As we'll discuss in the next chapter, cultural risks, people who don't want to join the "team" mindset, can bring down the morale of the entire team.

2. *People who don't get in their own way.* There are people who love their own ideas so much that they can't accept that someone else might have a better plan of action. Their own ego can get in the way of a management team moving forward. A common piece of important advice I hear from entrepreneurs of large companies

FIVE TEAM-BUILDING QUOTES THAT INSPIRE

"The strength of the team is each individual member.
The strength of each member is the team."
—Phil Jackson, former coach of the
championship Chicago Bulls and L.A. Lakers

"To be successful, you have to be out there, you have to hit the
ground running, and if you have a good team around you
and more than a fair share of luck, you might
make something happen."
—Sir Richard Branson, founder of the Virgin Group Ltd.

"A group becomes a team when each member is sure enough of
himself and his contribution to praise the skills of others."
—Norman Shidle, author of several business and communication books

"Your end goal is what can we do together to problem-solve?
I've contributed my piece, and then I step back."
—Laszlo Bock, senior vice president of people operations at Google

"Gettin' good players is easy.
Gettin' 'em to play together is the hard part."
—Casey Stengel, major league manager of the
New York Yankees for eight world titles

is that as you scale up, make sure you don't have a management team that gets in the way of each other. If you have too many people who love their own ideas too much and don't know when to step back, you start running on a treadmill.

3. *Humility.* If someone is able to be humble, own up to a mistake or a failed attempt at something, accept criticism and move forward constructively as part of a team, this is a big plus. People who can be humble can get stuff done, and, more than that, they are great team players.

Leaders vs. Victims

Team-building starts with hiring, which means evaluating people, and not just by their skills, or their GPA, or even their previous experience. You need to be able to assess who a person really is—their personality, their characteristics, and even their passions and how they will fit in with your plans, your dreams, and your goals.

The best way that I have found to do this is to conduct thorough back-channel reference checks. I'm not talking about the three or four people the candidate gives you to call, I'm talking about finding people who have managed and reported to this person in the past. LinkedIn is a great platform to find these people. I like to ask the back-channel references questions like, "What is the candidate's biggest blind spots? Would you work with this person again? Is this person a culture keeper or a cultural threat? How does this person deal with conflict? Was this person respected in XYZ company?" You will typically learn a lot more about a candidate by talking to people who worked with them in the past than simply by sitting down and having a one-hour chat with the candidate.

There are plenty of answers to the question: What makes a leader? But, for me, it's simply this: Leaders are people who, when they encounter a problem, adversity, or a barrier, immediately try to find a way to overcome it. They are proactive people who don't need a lot of guidance, they just get things done. Leaders talk about and execute ideas. They do this alone or collectively, whatever it takes. They see a problem and look for a new solution. When they fail, they look for other ways to succeed. They look toward the future, and no matter what has transpired, they always want to move forward, even if the path ahead of them is unclear. Leaders seek out new ways to do things rather than harping on what does not work.

Conversely, a victim is a person who, when they encounter adversity, a setback, or an obstacle, is programmed to point the finger and say, "It's not my fault." It's always someone else's fault. In football, I encountered it in the locker room from a constantly negative player saying things like, "Our coach is a moron," "The offensive coordinator doesn't know what he's doing," or "Our game plans suck." In business, victims feed on office politics, take a defeatist attitude, and follow the crowd—even if that crowd is not heading in a positive direction. Victims do not look for new ideas and will criticize without offering a better solution.

You may be wondering how this relates to failure. It's simple: If you have not embraced failure in a positive manner, learned from it, and reprogrammed your ego to your own intrinsic motivation, it is much harder to become a successful leader. If you view failure negatively, or cling to it, you are far more likely to emerge as a victim and use blame to shield you from admitting a mistake. Any time we're hiring at Integrate, we want to know what happened to the candidate at his or her previous company. If the person lost their job, why did the company let them go? We know that people are downsized all the time, but we want to hear how the person perceived the experience. For example, sometimes people go on and on and on about "The company had no idea what they were doing" . . . "My boss was a moron" . . . "The company will never make it" . . . etc. Those types of employees will say the same thing about your company if you hire them and it ultimately doesn't work out.

Granted, in many cases they may be simply stating a fact, but in my opinion a good leader with humility would describe the situation much differently by saying things like, "The organizational design didn't fit with the type of company I want to work for" or "It never felt like we could lock arms and build a unified culture" or "The values of the company were in conflict with what I believe to be true north."

Anyone Can Stop Being a Victim

What if you're realizing that perhaps it's you who behaves as a victim? That's okay, because we have all been a victim once or twice in our lives. So how can we get better? It's simple: Take ownership. Don't be afraid to say, "Yes, I screwed that one up . . . my fault, I'll make sure it doesn't happen again." And if you work in an organization or with people who don't understand and respect the fact that everyone makes a mistake, you should consider finding another place of employment.

Many people fall into patterns of always blaming others. If you recognize the pattern, you can then start to work on it. I remember falling into the victim mentality early in my skiing career. I felt like I was skiing better than my competitors and blamed the internal politics of the U.S. Ski Team as the reason I was not allocated more World Cup starts. From the time I was 15 until I was almost 18, I sat stagnant on the U.S. team, and I couldn't stand it.

That frustration drove me to train even harder than I ever thought possible, but because I still believed it was them and not me, mentally I was conditioning myself to think like a victim. What I learned later is that there is only really one cure for politics: winning. I learned to use my frustrations as motivation, but to not allow them to shape my thinking. I learned not to slip into the mindset of blaming others for my lack of progress.

Of course, it's often easier to see such patterns in other people than in ourselves. One of the most common types of victims we see all the time is the person who is always late but has an excuse . . . it was the traffic, the phone rang, the elevator was too slow, and on and on. It's a classic victim mentality. They never stop to think that perhaps they have to find a solution and plan accordingly to be on time. My parents taught my brother, sister, and me at a young age that honesty was the only policy that would work with them. Their rule was that no matter what we did or how bad we screwed up, if we were honest with them we would never get in trouble.

If you identify someone as a victim, the first thing you should do is sit down and talk to him or her. People aren't born leaders or victims.

A victim with the right internal motivation, who is given constructive feedback, can mature into a leader.

Despite trying to weed out the victims, sometimes you will end up with someone who has the "victim mentality" on your team. Perhaps they have mastered the art of interviewing well or even start off with a very positive nonvictim approach. Their true colors, however, will surface when something goes wrong and they blame everyone and everything in sight for the miscue or mistake. If this becomes a regular response and they don't show improvement after you have given them feedback, you should cut ties immediately regardless of how great the person is at their job. As an owner, CEO, or leader, you can't let the victim mentality impact the rest of your team or organization.

One of my favorite stories of taking a proactive stance, rather than being a victim, occurred shortly after I started Integrate. In our first year, I hired a remote-working employee to do sales in Maryland. Let's call him Demps. After about five months on the job, I could see that it was not working out. At that time, I did most of the hiring and all of the firing. So I called him, thanked him for his efforts, and let him know that I had decided to go in a different direction. I added that I'd be happy to write him a great letter of recommendation.

FROM VICTIM TO LEADER

An incredible story of moving from being a victim to becoming a leader comes from Candy Lightner. Her world was shattered when her 13-year-old daughter Laura was killed walking to a carnival, the victim of a drunk driver, a repeat DUI offender. Devastated, Lightner could have remained a victim, wallowing in the pain and blaming the world for her tragic loss. Instead, Lightner took the position of a leader. She went on to form Mothers Against Drunk Driving (MADD), which became a nationally recognized organization. Through education and legislation, MADD has had a significant impact on lowering the number of drunk-driving fatalities in America.

There was silence, which to me, felt like an eternity. Then he said, "Oh, really," which usually doesn't mean things are going to go well. Demps continued with a suggestion, "How about this . . . You can take away my base salary and all of my commissions, but I'm not leaving. I believe in this company and I have no doubt in my mind that I am going to kill it here." I was floored by his response. I remember thinking to myself, "This is a guy I would go to war with." We worked out the particulars to keep him onboard, and three years later, Demps has been the highest profit-generator in the company for 24 consecutive months, building the most profitable division inside the entire company.

I've told that story to CEOs with 30 years of experience, and none of them had ever heard of something like that. Demps refused to be a victim and was out to prove me wrong—and prove himself right. That was an extreme example, but now, when I'm hiring, I try to find people with the same DNA of a Demps.

CHAPTER EIGHT

LOCKING ARMS: BUILDING A UNIFIED CULTURE

When I co-founded Integrate, I was still relatively new to the business world, so I followed my co-founder's lead when it came to establishing a corporate culture. He had accumulated years of business experience during my years of competitive athletics. What he established, however, was a secretive organization where many things would never be discussed, including everything from employee ownership stakes in the company to how the company was really doing, and more. It was not a culture that I particularly cared for. I didn't feel that the people in our organization had a grasp of what was really going on inside the very company they were working for.

When I later became CEO, the very first thing I addressed was changing the company to a "transparency by default" culture. We aim to be fully transparent with our employees about everything from our financials to stock options, board decks, and sales. I continue making changes, since a business culture is always a work in progress in a living, breathing office environment. I had learned from my experiences with two NFL franchises how much of a difference a great culture could make on an organization and recognized the need to build a strong business culture for the future of our employees.

Building a strong culture within a team is at the core of success. I believe that you want a culture that recognizes and embraces shared values, attitudes, standards, and beliefs that characterize the goals of the organization. And it's a good idea to make sure it suits the best people who work at the company while making a positive impression on customers and anyone else associated with the business.

The idea of a closed-off, stuffy corporate culture was blown up by the tech boom when leaders recognized, and began to quantify, how a strong work-life integration resulted in a better bottom line. Happier, fulfilled, engaged employees were simply more productive than disgruntled, uninformed workers who were chained to their desks. Ping-pong tables started popping up in the lobbies of startups, collegial cafes and break rooms replaced cold, bring-your-own-lunch rooms, and as a result, businesses like Google, Facebook, and YouTube broke down the barriers between management and employees. Everyone locked arms.

These new cultures and their values, with far fewer boundaries, are a far cry from those of previous generations. Veteran entrepreneur, NYU Stern School of Business professor, and founder of CultureIQ Greg Besner points to the generational shift that is changing the perception of business and has brought culture to the foreground. "Our grandparents' generation of workers had such different career aspirations from today's generation. In the wake of bread lines and world wars, finding a career with long-term stability and fair income was a high priority," Besner says. "But today, the youngest of some 78 million baby boomers are turning 50, and the oldest baby boomers are retiring."

In contrast, the new generation of some 80 million Millennials, those born in the 1980s and 1990s, now entering the workforce, has grown up during times of economic growth and tremendous technological advancement. Rather than looking for a job that might someday become a career, they are, as Besner puts it, "placing great significance on the qualitative elements of their career, such as a positive company culture." Rather than retiring with a gold watch after 25 years of service, this generation will have likely changed jobs once if not twice during the first 25 months of employment. Reed Hastings, CEO of Netflix, told me that he doesn't even recognize tenure at the company. Instead, he lionizes performance. Period.

When a 2013 report published by Gallup, called "The State of the American Workplace," identified that 70 percent of American workers are disengaged at work, many business owners took notice and some recognized that they needed to pay closer attention to their company culture if they wanted to stay competitive during this demographic shift in the workplace.

Results of the new cultural awakening in recent years can be seen by the Great Place to Work Institute's annual list of the 100 best companies to work for. The list is topped by companies such as Google, NetApp, Microsoft, and Kimberly Clark, all of which feature very low turnover, high employee growth and job satisfaction, as well as some amazing revenues. In his book *The Cultural Cycle*, professor James L. Heskett notes that an "effective culture can account for 20 to 30 percent of the differential in corporate performance when compared with 'culturally unremarkable' competitors."

"Culture is like a hairstyle: Everyone has one, even if they're bald.
You can either pursue a style that accurately reflects your personality,
or you can pretend it doesn't matter and end up looking
like Edward Scissorhands."

—DREW MCLELLAN, HEAD OF AGENCY MANAGEMENT INSTITUTE

Creating a Culture That Works

Most of the best business cultures do not start accidentally or come about organically, by chance. They start at the top but are not top-down environments. They come from CEOs who are *not* convinced that their way is the only way, but instead understand that leadership means bringing together the talents, ideas, and abilities of an entire team of diverse individuals. I experienced this in Pittsburgh under head coach Mike Tomlin, as discussed in Chapter 7. His brand of team culture brought everyone together.

Establishing a culture you believe in, as I've learned, means having a clear and consistent vision and knowing how you would like everyone, inside and outside, to view the company. Many old-school CEOs and leaders were often "business operations first and people second." But it is the people that make a business successful. The greater inclusion of people in the operation of the business has led to far more significant contributions by employees, which spill over to more appreciation from customers. So unless you are alone with nothing but technology, your business is built around people producing products and providing services for other people.

The assumption that people should come first seems obvious. With that in mind, in all my efforts to create a team of leaders and not victims, I wanted to integrate into a culture in which we had transparency, one in which everyone in our company knew what was going on at all times, for better and for worse. I never felt the need to provide only good news and shield people from bad news. In time, bad news will spread regardless of your efforts to hide it. People will then feel betrayed if they find out from others; nobody likes being kept in the dark.

It's a good idea to start by sitting down with your board of directors or co-founders to write down what your core values are and how you want to weave them into the DNA of your team. It's important that the founders uphold the culture from the very beginning. To do so, the culture has to be more than just a shared vision. If you have a vision without a strategy it will never be more than a vision.

I first met Tony Bates at a United States Olympic Team fundraising event at the Yellowstone Club in Montana. Tony took over as GoPro's president in 2014 and is seen as one of the best culture builders there is. His advice to me is that I need to relate vision to pragmatic steps. "I think a strategy along with a vision cannot be understated," explains Tony. "Vision can be ambiguous, so having your vision linked to a strategy is very important. When I am coaching the team, I draw this on the board so they can see the need to shape their vision to where they want to go."

Personally, I also believe that it is okay to reach out a little bit beyond everyone's comfort zone when setting up a culture. I think it's good to feel a little bit uncomfortable—it's a sign we're all doing the right thing. For example, it's not traditional to share as much about our financials as we do with our employees. Admittedly, it can feel a bit uncomfortable, but in the end I would rather retain an employee who wants to work harder to solve problems than one who runs away from them.

Bates adds that in a good culture, it's important to take calculated risks and allow people to enjoy some latitude rather than holding them back. "Before going to Cisco, I worked for a large service provider where I was getting ready to do my first big pitch to executives and was told what I could and couldn't say," says Tony. "I was scared to begin with, and it was so debilitating. I vowed never to work in a culture like that again, and even left the company."

"On the flip side, if a leader does want to have a high-performance organization and a strong culture, they will recognize that it is a collaborative effort," says CultureIQ's Greg Besner, adding that building a culture can include participation by employees in committees and clubs within the overall office culture. He also adds that collecting feedback from employees on engagement surveys, and then communicating that feedback on the areas the company needs to address, helps promote a culture that focuses not only on financial results, but also one that recognizes the significance of nonfinancial results.

Cultural Cornerstones

There is no one-size-fits-all corporate culture. It will vary depending on a number of factors, including the type of business, size of the company, background of the founders and management team, and even the design of your facility. Following are some of the things I believe to be the cornerstones of a solid business culture.

Transparency

By now you should know how much I believe in transparency. At Integrate, we go over all of the key metrics of the business with the entire company. The goal is for all employees to feel they know the thinking, responsibilities, and strategy at various levels of the company and can share ideas and feedback no matter who they are.

Another thing that we do at Integrate to help bring more transparency into the organization is what we call a TGIF. I got this idea from Google. Every Friday Google holds a town-hall type of meeting where any employee in the Mountain View office can ask questions to Larry Page and Sergey Brin.

Our TGIF calls are based on this idea. They take place every other Friday and are all-hands calls. Everyone in the company can participate and ask questions. Since people often feel intimidated or uncomfortable in an any-question-welcome situation, we built a private forum on the Integrate server where employees can ask anonymous questions. Sometimes the calls even make me uncomfortable, especially when someone is discussing something I implemented or someone I brought onboard, but I think that's a good thing because it pushes me to maintain a culture where we put everything out there so nobody feels there are secrets or surprises.

While the TGIF calls work for us, they might not be right for every organization. As I mentioned earlier, there is no one-size-fits-all culture in business. Each company will need to determine what works best for them. But even if you choose an open, transparent culture, be careful when it comes to divulging too much information about your team. Transparency can be a good thing for your business, but we never cross the line into personal privacy and do our best to limit public scrutiny.

Time to Disconnect

I really believe, as do Eric Roza of Datalogix and Brad Feld of the Foundry Group, that people need time off. We all need to hit the

BEING GOOD STEWARDS OF THE DATA

If you subscribe to the notion of transparency by default, you will want to be clear with your employees that with that transparency comes the responsibility of being good stewards of the data. Confidential data must remain in-house and is not for public consumption. With transparency comes a need for mutual trust. There are no exceptions, and transition of the information past company walls is a firing offense.

reset button once in a while. People cannot come in early and leave late every single day without getting burnt out at some level. While you want employees to have a work-hard founder's mentality, you need to recognize the work-life integration that exists and how significant it is to make sure you have personally fulfilled, clear-thinking people.

I know how important time off is for me. It allows everyone to recharge and hit the refresh button. We have unlimited vacation days at Integrate, as do many other startups. By paying attention and maintaining a quantitative perspective about what is going on at the company, you can weed out anyone who is taking advantage of this, or any other, policy. If you build your team based on mutual respect and honesty, then the majority of people will respond in the same respectful manner. Those who are not respectful will be weeded out by their own actions.

Time off to balance work and life also translates into days or afternoons when someone needs to be with family or has a pressing problem that keeps them out of the office. It's important to understand that sometimes life will get in the way of business and everyone should be allowed to take care of pressing personal matters.

Empowerment and a Sense of Freedom

You empower people by *not* micromanaging. Our chief marketing officer, Scott Vaughan, and chief financial officer, David Tomizuka,

TAKE A NEEDED BREAK

Tony Schwartz, CEO of The Energy Project and author of *Be Excellent at Anything*, wrote in a 2013 *New York Times* article, "Daytime workouts, short afternoon naps, longer sleep hours, more time away from the office, and longer, more frequent vacations boosts productivity, job performance, and, of course, health." Schwartz backed up his words with research, including a Harvard study which estimated that sleep deprivation costs American companies $63.2 billion a year in lost productivity.

In another study from Oxford Economics, it was noted that Americans, collectively, left roughly 429 million unused paid days off on the table in 2013. "Leaving earned days on the table harms, not helps, employers by creating a less productive and less loyal employee," says Adam Sacks, president of the Tourism Economics division of Oxford Economics.

are both against micromanaging, so we err on the side of giving people general guidelines rather than explicit, detailed directions.

We also use the OKR management system to qualitatively measure our progress every quarter. OKR stands for Objectives and Key Results, a concept that was built inside of Intel and later put into practice at Google by John Doerr, one of Google's early investors. OKRs, or Key Performance Indicators (KPI), as other companies call them, help your company structure its goal setting. It starts by setting up an objective that is broad, something like improve product and rollouts. How would you measure that? That's where the key results come in. Two key results for that objective could be to successfully implement a QA process and a new product rollout protocol.

By using OKRs, we have quarterly, measurable goals. We keep everyone's OKRs on our internal online network, and we print a quarterly playbook that includes OKRs of the company and each employee. This way, we can all see what went well and what did not. One of the most important aspects of the OKRs is that they are not used as performance tools or for the purposes of evaluations or promotions. They are used as a learning tool to help us determine where we succeeded at reaching our goals, where we fell down, and what we learned from each experience. People know what I am working on, what our CFO is working on, what their officemate is working on, and so on. There are no secrets around our main focus and objectives from the CEO to office assistants. By looking at their own OKRs and those of others, employees can measure personal and group progress and, as John Doerr puts it, stay "in step with each other." That, in turn, creates better communication; everyone knows where each person is in the process.

Informed employees are more involved and empowered in a company. And the more freedom people have to take on tasks, manage them, find solutions, and execute them, the more they feel connected to and woven into the company's culture.

Physical Space

If you haven't watched Susan Cane's TED Talk on introverts, I highly recommend it. She opened my mind to the idea that American businesses are built for extroverts, down to the floor plans of our office spaces. This inspired me to get to know my employees better because although open spaces are great for some, other people need to be able to close the door to be at their most productive. We have several offices with a variety of floor plans. For example, in Boston our space has inner offices where anyone can shut the door if they want to do so. In Denver and Phoenix we have a mixture of open space and closed offices.

It's important to consider the comfort level of your employees before you decide how to lay out space or what type of office space to lease.

Talking to Customers and Employees

At different points in a company's maturation process, you are almost guaranteed to go through weeks or even months where you feel lost. Organizations deal with these periods in many different ways. Some hold closed-door working sessions to try to solve the problem inviting only top management. Other companies open up communication and ask for broader input.

KNOW WHAT MATTERS MOST

As your culture grows, it's a good idea to familiarize yourself with what matters the most to the people with whom you work.

A survey conducted by public relations firm Burson-Marsteller, in conjunction with the Great Place to Work Institute, of senior executives from top-ranked companies in the global workplace ratings yielded the following results:

Companies with the highest ratings:

▷ Invested more time in their employees, including work-life programs, flex time, health benefits, and perks;

▷ Are upgrading, offering more programs with stability and career development opportunities;

▷ Recognize that culture is critical to talent retention.

One way we try to solve problems at Integrate is by talking to our customers. It's a concept that was instilled in me by David Karnstedt, who I talked about in Chapter 6.

When you haven't nailed a product market fit or you're having challenges relating to your product or corporate vision, the natural tendency is to look inside the company and turn your attention to where you or your team went wrong. You might talk to your VP of product, to the CFO, your board of directors, or your sales team. However, over the past four years, whenever we've been stuck at Integrate, I always come back to that one key principle that David taught me: Go talk to your customers.

"I go out to talk to customers because a) you want to understand what works and what doesn't work in the product; b) it helps you refine your approach and know how you are going to market it; and c) probably the most important thing is it fires you up. You get a lot of enthusiasm from being out there with customers and talking to people about your product," David told me.

Today, part of our culture at Integrate is to find out what our customers think, and need, and then work to meet their needs. It sounds fairly obvious, but it is surprising how easy it can be to forget that, especially when you feel stuck.

"I find that as a CEO, or as an executive, it's easy to get so wrapped up in the minutia and the day-to-day operations that you are not out on the front lines as a leader," says David. "So many leaders that I know never go out and talk to their employees without an agenda. I used to schedule time just to walk the halls and get a pulse on how the culture is doing, how the employees are doing, and build and develop relationships. It's much different than a quarterly all-hands meeting, which is not the same as talking to someone and asking how it's going. Making personal connections makes such a difference."

I couldn't agree more. It's one of the reasons why you, as an entrepreneur, executive, or CEO, enjoy coming to work every day.

Your Organizational Design

Organizational design, simply put, is the processes, structure, and hierarchy you put into place that allow you to put your culture into practice. It's "how you do things." This will include your communication, company policies, team building, performance indicators, performance evaluations, division of responsibilities, and even how you schedule, and run, meetings. For example, do you have a weekly meeting at the same time and in the same place or do you hold meetings only when there is something worthy of discussing at a meeting? Are meetings for all employees, division heads, or certain team members? Do you always meet in conference rooms, in a specific area of the office, or by conference calls, or does the setting change? Do you schedule meetings outside the office on occasion?

If designed well, everyone in the business can do his or her job more effectively. Your business culture will significantly be enhanced if the organizational design you put into place clarifies authority, responsibility, and accountability. In our case, the OKRs help in that regard. It is important, as well, to determine your management strategy (i.e., top-down or bottom-up? Yours may be 50–50, 60–40, 70–30, and so on). Some corporate cultures have management making most major decisions, while others have everyone involved in all decisions. It's up to each business to determine what works best for them.

One of the most important factors in any organizational design, though, is communication. It is also one of the most difficult parts to get right. In theory, the design should define the methods of communications that will be most direct, accessible, and effective for everyone. People tend to believe that the easy and most inclusive method is to do all communication electronically. However, we know that the tone of email is easily misinterpreted—and that can lead to a breakdown in culture.

Optimism Delusion

If you're a person who tends to see the glass half full, it can be easy to fall into something called the optimism delusion—and for leaders, it doesn't always work for the long haul. In fact, it can also cause a breakdown in culture. The idea is that there is a pressure to only share the good news with your team because by sharing the bad news it will kill the company's morale. You try to present a picture that "everything is terrific" while sweeping bad news under the rug. In reality, I believe this is the exact opposite of the right way to build a strong, healthy, solid culture.

By standing up and saying, "Hey, we're getting our butts kicked by XYZ company," or "Hey, we just lost a client because this area of the product is not working," we are being honest and bringing everyone into the real environment to help solve the problem. Sometimes you have to be honest and let people know that if, as a team, we don't resolve the issues, there are going to be major problems.

These types of conversations are healthy to have because they build trust and you will find out very quickly who your best teammates are. If you keep presenting everything as positive, and sweeping everything negative under the rug, eventually the rug will become a hill and people

DON'T DEMOTIVATE YOUR EMPLOYEES

There are four ways to totally demotivate your employees. The "don't do this" list:

1. *Publicly criticize.* I learned this one the hard way. In sports, it is normal to be criticized in front of your peers when you drop a pass or throw an interception. However, I tried it once in business and the employee quit two weeks later. Criticism is best served in a one-to-one environment by using the "chiropractic method." Massage first with some positive feedback and then crack and realign with the constructive feedback.

2. *Neglect spending one-on-one time with your team.* HR studies show that managers who don't spend time individually with their team members are much more likely to lose an employee.

3. *Fail to provide praise.* When someone does a great job, they want to know that people see it. If they don't, the employee will wonder why they are working so hard. But when giving praise, make it specific so it does not sound patronizing.

4. *Use fear-based motivation.* This can make an employee think more about their job security than doing their actual job.

will start falling off the rug or looking underneath it only to discover that things are not as good as they seem.

In the end, whether it's 48 hours, ten seconds, or whether you are by yourself or working with a team, the major keys to success are being able to:

▷ Accept your new reality;
▷ Set a deadline for the emotional acceptance stage;
▷ Extract what you have learned;
▷ Move on.

Hiring to Match Your Culture

Laszlo Bock of Google believes in hiring emergent leaders who are able to step up at the right time and also step back when necessary. They are the ones that fight feverishly when they feel strongly about something but also possess enough humility to acknowledge that they were wrong when presented new supporting facts. Greg Besner, while recognizing that there is sometimes a need for highly trained, experienced specialists in some areas, also says that he favors hiring "great people over great resumes and great experience." Personally, I would never hire someone that I believed to be a culture risk, regardless of his or her competency.

Chad Hurley, co-founder of YouTube, introduced me to Bill Maris in 2009 at TEDMED. Bill is the president and managing director of Google Ventures and is responsible for all of Google's venture investing. Bill and I bonded over our mutual passion for taking better care of the oldest people living in our world today. He's one of the biggest supporters in the nonprofit I started, Wish of a Lifetime, and I consider him one of my closest friends.

Bill, who has played a leading role in Google Ventures' 250-plus investments, says that he selects where to put the investment dollars based largely on the person behind the business, even more significantly than their experience or the specific businesses they're trying to launch.

These ideas all make good sense to me, and I have tried to drill them down into the DNA at Integrate. The right people are keys to any organization, and it's not simply about their resume. As I discussed in the previous chapter, your hiring decisions are among the most important decisions you will make. In this chapter, I shed some light on some attributes that I think are important for the sake of the culture.

Along with emergent leadership, humility and respect are also part of being on a team. People should inherently care about those with whom they work. This is true at all levels from top management to interns. If people have an unhealthy amount of disrespect for one another, the likelihood that the entire organization will have a difficult time achieving a desirable culture will increase. In addition, you also want to have people who have some positive sense of the founder's mentality or ownership.

GET A PULSE ON YOUR CULTURE

"The world is becoming a smaller place, and when you look around the office you'll likely see people of various ages, from all socioeconomic backgrounds and from all parts of the world," says Greg Besner of CultureIQ. "That's what makes it so important that the communication, the collaboration, the support network, and the workplace environment all tie together as part of your culture. It is part of the reason culture has become such a topic of interest for so many businesses and business leaders."

Over the past couple of years, Besner and his team have focused on developing software to help companies build and monitor the business culture within their office. Using a series of anonymous surveys administered by CultureIQ, feedback from employees is collected and measured. The results can be used to help strengthen a business's existing culture. Data is quantified and the software provides a dashboard for the company to see the metrics, comments, and trends, as well as review nine categories and associated qualities common to high-performance organizations. They are:

▷ Ownership

▷ Agility

▷ Support

▷ Mission and Value Alignment

▷ Innovation

▷ Environment

▷ Performance Orientation

▷ Collaboration and Communication

▷ Wellness

GET A PULSE ON YOUR CULTURE, continued

By understanding how your company is performing in these areas, you can evaluate your business culture and see where improvements can be made. The company also offers a library of programs to explore and implement as you try to strengthen company culture.

As a business owner, CEO, or manager, you want to find out how the culture you've created is working. Through research, surveys, and even one-one conversations, you want to be able to answer questions such as:

▷ Do people in your office come to work just for the paycheck or do they really believe in the vision, the products, and the goals of the business?

▷ Do they understand, and care about, the daily pain and challenges the business faces?

▷ Do they understand, and care about, the pain and challenges the customer faces?

▷ Are they active in improving the culture and offer ideas and feedback?

While team members typically do not have the same stake in the business as the managers, owners, or shareholders, they should have a sense that this is their company too and not just a place to spend eight or nine hours a day.

The final quality employees should have, as mentioned in the previous chapter, is competency. While I consider emerging leadership, humility, and a sense of ownership (or founder's mentality) to be more significant for creating the right culture, you still need people who know what they are doing. This does not necessarily come from someone's GPA or resume. It comes from his or her background and from what they have learned along the way.

CHAPTER NINE

THE ROLLER-COASTER RIDE

One month before NFL training camp, I was returning a kickoff at the end of practice and I felt a pop in my hamstring. I fell to the ground and immediately knew something was wrong. I limped off the field and into the training room. An MRI showed that I had a two-centimeter tear of my semimembranosus muscle at the top of my hamstring. The doctor told me that I didn't need surgery and if I took a week off I should be good to go. The first time I sprinted, about a week later, I felt it tear again. The challenge of a hamstring injury for a sprinter is that you never know when it's fully healed.

It was the first time in my athletic career that I had to deal with being sidelined by an injury. It was bad enough not being on the field, but the climate in the NFL for a rookie that is injured is difficult. You get a lot of pressure from the team, the team physician, and the coaches, all of whom want you to get back on the field. There's even a saying in the NFL: "You can't make the club in the tub."

This was a very challenging time for me mentally because I wanted to be playing but my body wouldn't let me. The roller coaster had come down in an instant, and it was not going back up any time soon. It was nearly six months by the time my hamstring was strong enough to sprint on.

In sports, business, and life in general, we are all on a roller-coaster ride. And managing our own psychology through the ups and downs is one of life's great challenges.

Taking a Ride

There were many periods in my life where I had to learn how to better manage my own psychology, not just when I was hurt in the NFL.

When you have your own startup, it's typical to wake up feeling great about your product, your team, and your business and have little doubt that you are going to change the world. Then, later in the day, you get a few phone calls and find out that you are about to lose a major client or that the servers have completely gone down and you can't conduct any business.

Suddenly, that roller coaster drops and you begin to wonder how much longer your company will be around. One minute you're riding high, and the next minute you're at the bottom looking up.

In business, it rarely feels like clear sailing, and there are plenty of drops along the way. Because of that, I have a constant feeling that no matter how well we're doing, something can, and likely will, go wrong. Some people call it productive paranoia. It's a constant uneasy feeling in the back of your head; however, it's productive because it pushes you to work harder, pay closer attention, and make sure that you're always sweeping the corners or looking carefully at the incidentals. We are a data-driven company focused on the signs and signals, and we try to figure out what's working, what isn't, and where we want to do business. We take risks but not without doing our homework. We'll look at where the gaps are in our business and try to determine how to fill them in. The paranoia leads to being more aware and productive.

The Downward Turn

I subscribe to the policy of hoping for the best but always preparing for the worst. I remember a day early on at Integrate that served as a major wakeup call. At the time, my co-founder was running all of finance, and we got a call from our lender explaining that we had broken a loan covenant, and if it so desired, the bank could call all of the capital and make us repay the $7 million working cash flow loan immediately. We had a minimum cash balance requirement of $2 million, and we had dropped below $1 million. To make things worse, we unknowingly broke the covenant, which rarely happens. It was clear that we did not have the right financial controls in the business.

The business was literally about to fail because we had payroll coming up and not enough cash in the bank to survive. I immediately flew to Denver from San Francisco to meet with the bank. The only leverage that I had was to threaten the lender that I was going to shut down the business and everyone was going to lose if they did not modify the borrowing base and extend us a $2 million bridge loan until we could close the new equity round that we were working on. It was contentious at times, but it worked. They extended the bridge loan and forgave the broken covenant, and I successfully raised $6 million from our existing investors.

Of course, no one was happy with us. I'll never forget meeting with the Comcast partnership and taking a deserved tongue-lashing from Amy Banse, who runs their team. You might be asking yourself how we could possibly have not known that our cash dropped below the minimum balance and why I didn't get in front of the problem instead of reacting behind it. It's simple: The problem was never reported to me or my co-founder, and our controller was in way over his head; he didn't understand the mechanics of the loan and didn't keep track appropriately. I can't stress enough to any entrepreneur the importance of hiring competent financial leaders from the very

WHEN THE BUBBLE BURSTS

Prior to his position as the CEO of Skype or his current role as president of GoPro, Tony Bates learned the ups and downs of business during the dotcom boom of the late 1990s and the subsequent crash of 2001.

"It was early on in my tenure at Cisco Systems . . . we were having the time of our life with the boom of the internet, and I was working on the high-end router products," says Tony. "Obviously, when the bubble burst, it had a big impact on Cisco and made us realize how quickly things could change. It was a major learning experience for me. We had reached a point where we were actually the number-one largest market cap company for one day. Exxon was number two. What's interesting is that when you're in the middle of something like that, it's very hard to recognize that it's a bubble that can burst.

"I believed everything they were saying about the dotcom industry because I was part of it and part of helping to build it. I remember being at a leadership conference and people were talking about how we could actually go to a trillion dollars in market cap! I remember walking out of that leadership conference and saying, 'Okay, I'm in and all ready to go.' Then, when it all went crazy, I remember asking myself, 'How did I really buy into that when it made no sense?'

"It was a significant lesson for me, learning to become more objective and much more long term in my thinking, rather than getting caught up in the short term—it's really an important perspective. Often the way people learn is by experiencing a big shock in some way. That taught me a lot about leadership. That was the first time I experienced such a crash, and I had to make really tough budget decisions, the kind that test your leadership capabilities on a human and strategic level.

"I guess I passed the test, but knew that I never want to be caught in such a situation again."

beginning of the business. Our failure to do so almost cost us the business.

Not unlike failing, such a plunge can also provide some excellent lessons. While I can't say I'm glad it happened, I will say that it did provide me with much greater insights into the financial end of the business, and I have since been much more aware of where we stand financially.

Managing Risk

Every business venture means taking a risk. As soon as you open your doors or launch your website you are taking a risk. What if there isn't a big enough market for your product? What if it will be too expensive and difficult to reach your target demographic? What if a competitor beats you to the punch?

There are plenty of "what ifs" in business that can take you on a wild ride if you do not cover all of your bases through researching, testing, and, as mentioned earlier, talking with the important people around you, especially your customers. In addition, you want to keep tabs on your industry on a daily basis and know what your competitors are up to.

One of the first things I did as CEO was make a promise to myself that I would not take unnecessary risks. I wanted us to mature from a "fly by the seat of our pants" type of business to leveraging data to help us make more informed and calculated decisions. At times of bad news one of my board members and mentors, Seth Levine, always says, "1. Don't panic. 2. Gather information. 3. Make informed decision." Sometimes the urge is to be reactive to bad news and want to act immediately on it. But it's much more effective to take a step back, look at the information objectively, and then put a plan of action in place.

Tuning Out the Noise

I talked about drowning out the noise when discussing intrinsic versus extrinsic motivation. It's also imperative when trying to focus on the path ahead of you in business. Having survived the whirlwind of negativity surrounding the bursting of the dotcom bubble while at Cisco, Tony Bates now handles the ups and downs of the internet world without great anxiety.

"It helped me put it all into perspective," he says. "At Skype people would read about what others were saying and say, 'We've already won, we've destroyed the telecommunication industry,' which, first of all, wasn't true, we only disrupted it. Secondly, I reminded people that it's just one of many innings and that great companies are always in marathons, they're not in sprints."

Tony believes you should have filters in place for much of the reporting you read and hear. "Tuning out the noise is a good strategy but hard to implement in reality," Tony told me, adding that it's important to make a list of the right people to pay attention to. This would include:

1. Customers
2. Employees
3. Shareholders

"All of the others you try to block out," Tony advises.

But, he says, it's also something to remember when you have to filter your own message. "One of my lowest moments was when I was at Skype and we made some management changes," Tony recalls. "There was a headline that basically said that we let them go because we didn't want to pay them out. Of course this got a lot of press and a lot of emotional responses in the Valley. It was a complicated situation, but what I didn't realize was that I didn't do enough to get the full story out there, to explain what was really happening. If I had it to do over, I would have handled it much differently and explained the situation in greater detail." For entrepreneurs, getting their own message out early and often is crucial.

Also critical: Always stay current by doing your own research. Companies fall behind because they aren't staying on top of the marketplace. While much of the news, even in your industry, may be noise, hype, or even rumors, there is typically enough information about your competitors that you can review to keep you in the loop.

"You'd be surprised by how many people are not aware of the competition," says Tony. "If you know what's going on in your industry, you can react like a speedboat than an aircraft carrier if you see major events on the horizon. That way you can adjust."

Finding a Balance

Some people seem to have this genetic code where they are able to stay emotionally neutral at times of stress and victory. They remain even-keeled, or at least appear to do so at all times. In sports, you can take a look at New England Patriots coach Bill Belichick or San Antonio Spurs coach Gregg Popovich. In business there are also some pretty stoic figures.

I think this is one of the most important skills to master to be able to manage the ups and downs in life, business, and athletics. The objective is to work on your mind so you do not allow yourself to get too high or too low, especially if you're an emotional person. I've done a lot of work to try to get to a more even place, and though I've narrowed

LET ENDORPHINS HELP YOU

One of the ways I stay even mentally is through consistent exercise. It's an ideal way to let your body work for you. When you exercise, your body releases chemicals called endorphins. These endorphins reduce stress while also triggering a more positive feeling in the body. After a long workout or a long run, you can feel a sense of euphoria along with a more positive and energized outlook on life.

Exercise is a great way to remove yourself from the roller coaster of business, or any other areas of life that cause stress, but it's not something to do only when you are hitting low points. Exercise should become a constant in your life to help you stay on track and better able to withstand the bumps and bruises along the way.

the gap between the highs and the lows so I'm more stable, I have not perfected it by any means.

If it's something you struggle with, know that balancing starts with an understanding of why it is important to stay emotionally even. As I see it, the higher you are, the further you can fall, and that cycle of riding the emotional roller coaster and getting yourself up when you're down, and then going back down, is exhausting. As a result you expend too much energy and too much time overthinking the situation. This energy could be put to better use elsewhere.

The way each person achieves narrowing the emotional gap and trying to be more even is largely dependent on each person's personality.

When I was on the Steelers, Coach Tomlin would constantly tell us that he wanted a boring football team. "I want us to pack our lunch pails, get our work done, and go home without any of the flash. I want a boring-ass football team," he would say.

I didn't fully understand it then, but I think the sense of "boring" that Tomlin meant was the idea of being more steady and predictable. If you rein in the emotions and remain somewhat consistent every day, you may be a little more boring, but you will be predictable—and predictability works very well in business.

Companies working with predictable leadership have more consistency, and this also spills over outside of the organization where customers will know what to expect and what they can count on from your business.

In the End, It's All Worthwhile

You've probably seen kids, and adults for that matter, who are apprehensive waiting on line to ride a roller coaster. They aren't sure what they are in for, and some get onboard rather tentatively. Then, a few minutes later, the ride is over, and they leave smiling, glad they went. Whether they loved it or not, they will say, "I'm glad I had the chance to ride it."

When I asked Apolo Ohno what he thought about the roller-coaster ride, he said, "It's been awesome!" He's thankful to have been on board. "When I was 18 or 19 years old, I had the world at my fingertips, but I didn't have anybody to teach me what was coming up after sports," says Apolo, who was fortunate to stay on top of his sport for more than a decade.

"I learned, I made mistakes, and I have certainly been through the roller-coaster ride," adds Apolo. "I think if you just have one linear path of uphill progress it's kind of boring. No great athlete in the world has won every race or every title, not even the greatest of the greats . . . Michael Jordan, Michael Johnson, they had their failures. Without failures we don't learn for ourselves. Unfortunately in business it's not like there's another race coming up. You have to put so much into it, money, time, and so on, and you have to make sure you've got your bases covered. I think it's a lot more painful when you fail in a business, but you still have to rebound and start up that roller-coaster ride all over again, using what you've learned."

He's so right, as evidenced by all the entrepreneurs who have watched one company flounder or fail and the next one, or the one after that, take them up to the top of the mountain once again—or for the first time.

CHAPTER TEN

MAKE A DIFFERENCE:
DEFINING YOUR LEGACY

'm proud of it all, of each part of my life. Each piece has played a pivotal role in shaping the person I am today. Looking back at sports, my dreams of experiencing life in the Olympics and at the NFL level both came true.

But when all is said and done, we're all likely to be forgotten, no matter what sort of fame and fortune we had in life. I thought about that a lot as I traveled and saw people in different cultures around the world. I realized that I have been very fortunate and began to think about what my legacy would be . . . what would I be remembered for?

It was during my travels that I began to think that it should involve doing something for someone else. I wanted to help others reach their dreams.

Looking Outside Yourself

At some point in life it's important to step back and take a broader, bolder look at the world around us. What I saw was that for each person who has enjoyed great success, there are many others whose goals, dreams, and wishes go unfulfilled. Many people don't have the means necessary to achieve what others of us take for granted. I believe that each of us who has been fortunate and had many opportunities in life should make an effort to better the life of at least one other person, if not many.

The impetus to do something for others came largely from my mother. My dad has always been very driven to succeed, to win, and to be the best at whatever he did. He worked six days a week from dawn until dark to support the needs of our family. He was also the driving influence for me in athletics; he was my first football coach and my ski coach for a long time. More than anyone else in my life, he inspired me to become the best I could be. He was a state champion wrestler and a very good athlete in his own right growing up in Lower Merion, Pennsylvania, where he went to the same high school that Kobe Bryant later attended. While he was inspiring me, he also became very a successful clinical psychologist. Any time I am dealing with a complex issue in life, he's the first person I turn to.

My mom, too, loved and supported my dreams of becoming a successful athlete, she did not miss a single college football game that I played in, and would often travel the world to see me ski. However, she always told me, "I'm less concerned if you win a gold medal and care more about how you treat people and what you do to give back to the world." My mom is the ultimate nurturer. I believe that she was put on this world to love and take care of things and people. I am so lucky to have her as my mom. I had two incredible parents who helped shape my life, and they remain two of my best friends, biggest fans, and determined advocates.

I'm proud of what I was able to accomplish in athletics. But there is something more to a legacy, no matter what level of success someone has achieved. You don't have to be an Olympic athlete to have achieved success. The truth is that success comes from making changes in your

A FATHER'S TAKE: LARRY BLOOM

Two of the most valuable people in my life I did not have to seek out: my parents.

My dad has been there with me for the whole ride, up and down the mountains, through the agony of sitting on the sidelines with a long hamstring injury in football, and as I ride the roller coaster that is starting a business. Larry Bloom, a clinical psychologist for 40 years, saved me a bundle on therapy costs and has a lot to say about how I got where I am today.

I asked him to comment on my journey, through his own eyes.

"Starting at a young age, Jeremy demonstrated a great deal of talent, but along the way, whether it was in skiing, football, or track and field, he also experienced setbacks. Even though he was a high-achievement-oriented kid, he fell, stumbled and experienced a lack of achieving from time to time, as is the case when facing challenges.

"Under the circumstances, he had to learn to deal with it, and he did. You have to do so if you're going to get further up the ladder. You have to learn to deal with the failures and the realization that you won't always succeed. It's part of sports and part of business.

"There is also a need to know what you can and cannot control. I remember when Jeremy was vying to become one of three or four Americans to make the Olympic team in 2002. He had to go through the arduous process of competing. And no matter how well you do, it's not always clear whom the coaches are going to pick for the team. It's not necessarily objective. He called me from France one evening and said to me, 'Dad, I'm stressed. I don't know what they're going to do or how they're going to handle it.' I remember telling him, 'Jeremy, you are trying

A FATHER'S TAKE: LARRY BLOOM, continued

to control something you have no control over. You cannot control what the coaches are going to do or what discretionary choices they are going to make; all you have is control over yourself. So you have to push that away, get up tomorrow morning, and forget about what they are going to do . . . just get to the point where you are doing better every single day. That's all you focus on.'

"The other important aspect of Jeremy's careers is that he found people to turn to. It helps to have mentors and relationships with people whom you know well and trust. I would say learning how to deal with failures and setbacks, understanding what you can and cannot control, and building a network of people you can turn to are all important aspects of Jeremy's life that have helped him.

"Business doesn't always go as planned. We've had many conversations in recent years, and I know that getting involved in a startup means you're going to have hills and valleys. He approaches the business, the peaks and valleys and the setbacks, in the same way as he did in sports."

community, building a thriving small business, raising children you can be proud of, having your novel published, or affording the vacation home you've always wanted.

However, when it comes to a legacy, in my view, it is something that you build for somebody else, not for yourself. While I might inspire young athletes on the slopes or on the field, or young hires at Integrate, it's not the same as specifically doing things for other people.

One of the reasons I started a nonprofit, called Wish of a Lifetime, was because I was guilty of living the professional athlete selfish existence. To succeed as a collegiate or professional athlete, you have to do a lot of things that are deeply rooted in being selfish. You have to focus on yourself and do whatever it takes to accomplish your goals. It's so competitive that you can't focus elsewhere, and, in large part because of that, you end up being selfish. At the time you don't even realize it because you are so focused on reaching your goal and blocking out the outside world.

My Inspiration for Helping Seniors

My attention gravitated toward seniors largely because of my grandmother and my grandfather. For most of us, inspiration to give back—in small and large ways—naturally comes from that which is closest to us, such as the people living with us. When I grew up, my mom's mother, Donna, was living downstairs in our home. For the first 19 years of my life, it was my mom, dad, brother, sister, and my grandmother. She was like a second mother to me. Today, she's living in Keystone, Colorado, high in the Rocky Mountains, and at the age of 89 she still drives through the snow and ice to volunteer at the elementary school and at the local senior center. She has the most wonderful outlook on life, and although she has many challenges, I never hear her complain.

Meanwhile, my dad's father, who passed away in 2014, was one of my best friends growing up. When I was three years old he was my first ski instructor and would throw miniature-sized candy bars down the mountain to teach me how to ski. A huge Denver Broncos and Miami Dolphins fan, he also helped increase my passion for football.

At 17, I traveled to Asia for the first time for a World Cup skiing competition. I remember one afternoon as I was riding on a crowded bus, through the busy streets of Tokyo, a woman who appeared to be at least 80 years of age got on the bus, and nearly everyone who was seated stood up to politely offer her their seats. Then, as the bus started moving again, they each bowed to her. I was a bit awestruck by the reverence directed toward this elderly woman. Was she famous? No, she was simply being respected as one of their elders.

As I traveled around the world over the next decade, I saw similar acts of respect and kindness to seniors not only throughout Asia, but also in Scandinavian countries and elsewhere. It made me think about our country and how in some ways, we are completely backwards in the way we treat the oldest people in our society. We spend so much of our time focused on the youth, always looking for the up-and-comers, while often turning a cold shoulder to the people who gave us life, shaped our world, and fought wars to defend our freedom.

Starting a Nonprofit

Starting my own nonprofit was never a dream of mine. I turned down the idea of starting the Jeremy Bloom Foundation while I was playing sports because I felt the only reason my agents wanted me to launch it was for PR and marketing purposes. However, there wasn't another nonprofit that was granting wishes to the oldest people in our country on a large scale, so I decided to start Wish of a Lifetime in 2008. It has been the most meaningful journey of my life because the feeling of being a small part in helping a 90-year-old man or woman experience something that they have dreamed about their entire life is a feeling of purpose that I had never experienced before in athletics.

I had no idea what I was doing when I started. I was playing with the Steelers in the summer of 2008, and I had some time off prior to the pre-season. I filled out a 30-page IRS form used to apply for tax-exempt status (501(c)(3) status).

The process after that isn't as daunting as it seems, although it does take some time. Even at a small, community-based level, it's possible to start and run a small nonprofit focused on whatever matters most to you. About six months later, we were approved and could begin accepting tax-free donations. During the approval process I started building a board of directors and created bylaws for the organization. Then I planned a visit to an existing organization that worked with seniors so I could figure out what people at this age would wish for. One of my early board members, Laura Wildt, hooked me up with the Volunteers of America charity, which has a program to help senior citizens find children to mentor. It was a good place to start; it gave me the opportunity to meet seniors and get to know them.

It was there that I met a woman named Nancy Tarpin. Nancy had no idea who I was or why I was there, but we struck up a conversation about our families and about growing up in Colorado during different generations. She was a very low-income senior, 86 years old, but still active in her community. And she was very engaging. At one point, I asked her what her one wish in life was, if she could do anything she wanted. She told me that her daughter Lucille was living in Arizona and had been diagnosed with ovarian cancer ten years before. She had not seen her daughter in more than a decade, as she didn't have the money to make the trip. She told me that it tore her heart out to know that she was going to lose her daughter without being able to say goodbye. I was floored. Here I was, traveling around the world as a skier and football player, born into an opportunity-rich family, able to support all my dreams. And there was a sweet woman living one short flight away from a daughter who was fighting for her life, and this woman didn't have the means to spend time with her.

One week later, Nancy and I were on a flight to Arizona. I drove her to Claypool, Arizona, where we met Lucille at a Denny's. I said hello to Lucille and dropped Nancy off to spend time with her. Three days later I drove back up to Claypool. Nancy was a completely different woman. She was smiling from ear to ear and didn't stop smiling all the way back to Denver. Nancy is normally a very quiet person. But the entire way back to Colorado, I don't think there was a moment of silence. She told me every detail of her trip.

It was such a powerful experience, not only for her but also for me. Truthfully, it was one of the most powerful experiences of my life. In that moment, I had played a small part in changing somebody's life, even for a brief time. It hadn't cost much to do it, either. I had never done something like that before. In the past, all my goals were centered on myself, winning gold medals and football games. At the time I was contemplating returning to skiing to compete in my third Olympics in Vancouver, Canada. However, after my experience with Nancy I remember calling my mom and telling her that I had found my new mission in life and that this foundation was going to have a huge impact on many people's lives. I retired the next week from the U.S. Ski Team, and for the next two years, before I started Integrate, Wish of a Lifetime was my sole focus.

Growing Pains

We started small. I seeded Wish of a Lifetime with $25,000 and hired a part-time executive director, Patrick Sablich, to work with me. We didn't open an office; we worked out of coffee shops to start. The nonprofit was the first chapter in my post-athletic career, and I learned a lot of great lessons. In starting a nonprofit I mixed up a few steps. And if I were to start another one in the future, there are things I would change.

One of the errors in judgment was that I thought that my name recognition and notoriety would automatically translate into donations and support. My game plan was to build a website, then go on TV to talk about the new cause and play up a fundraiser that I planned to have. And I did just that. I received a lot of nice emails wishing us luck, but not a single ticket was sold. We cancelled the fundraiser.

Talk about fueled by failure . . . I was now more determined than ever to make this happen. The mistake that I made was not recognizing that it takes a grass-roots effort to build a nonprofit from the ground up. In the beginning stages there is nothing more important than creating a good board of directors. It's more important than your website and more important than your marketing. You have to start by building an operational board, which could be five to fifteen people, depending on the scope of the projects you hope to accomplish. This will be your "staff," and you have to be upfront with these people, letting them know that you're going to need their services in various capacities from providing advice to planning events to helping you scale the nonprofit. Whatever they can do, you'll need it, especially networking—that's where the fundraising comes from, I learned.

It's hard to get people to jump onboard, but fortunately I found 12 people, including a financial expert, a marketing expert, a legal expert, several high-net-worth individuals, and some worker bees who had free time to dedicate to the mission. In a nonprofit, time is a very valuable commodity. As important is making sure that the people you choose are engaged in the mission for similar reasons. Each of my board members was committed to the mission; they had stories to tell about how they too believed that the senior population had done so much for us and still had so much more to give.

MISSION AND VISION STATEMENT

Wish of a Lifetime (WOL) envisions a world in which society embraces aging and the inherent wisdom that accompanies it, where seniors are celebrated for their accomplishments and sacrifices and where intergenerational connections are part of our daily life.

Our belief is that growing older doesn't mean you have to stop dreaming and living a life of purpose. Most elderly men and women have something in their life that they have always wanted to do or see, but for many different reasons they have not been able to live out these dreams.

By connecting seniors to people, purpose, and passions through the granting of their wishes, WOL is able to relieve the feelings of isolation that many seniors live with. WOL engages the hearts and minds of young and old alike by sharing our Wish Recipients' stories.

A year later, after we had all teamed up to network and let people know about Wish of a Lifetime, we held a fundraiser. This time I leaned on my board to sell 20 tickets each, so they went out and hit their networks, and with a month left to go, we sold out all 500 tickets!

After a very successful first fundraiser I was able to invest more and hire a few additional people. Once we gained traction locally in Colorado, I wanted to expand nationally without spending a lot of money on staffing, so I partnered with the largest senior living company in the United States, Brookdale Senior Living. But first I had to convince them that it was their social duty to grant wishes to their residents. I reached out to one of their vice presidents, Sara Terry, and requested a meeting. I flew to their Chicago headquarters and gave a two-hour presentation to her and her team. Sara and I hit it off from the very beginning; it felt like she was someone that I had known my whole life. She also believed deeply in our mission, and serendipitously Brookdale's corporate values mirrored our mission almost perfectly. At the end of the meeting we agreed in principle to a multiyear deal that would enable Wish of a Lifetime to expand nationally with a volunteer staff at Brookdale. The company became our founding sponsor and has helped us fund hundreds of wishes.

Today, Wish of a Lifetime has Jillaina Wachendorf as CEO. Jillaina comes from a business background as a member of the founding team at Starz Networks. She is one of the most energetic and passionate executives I have worked with in my life.

Jillaina had taken time off from corporate America to raise a family and discovered the joy of volunteering. "During my 'nonworking' years, I actually worked as much as ever. I volunteered in every capacity possible, for the school, the church, the community, and for most things that touched the lives of my kids. For me it was like a full-time job," says Jillaina, who also shares the larger vision of the foundation.

"Jeremy's goal with this organization is to really encourage all generations to respect and appreciate seniors and aging in general. We want to bridge generational gaps by sharing the story of our wish recipients who are living life purposefully and vitally," says Jillaina. "This can be someone experiencing an unfullfilled dream such as skydiving, reconnecting with loved ones or pursuing their passion or hobby from a wheelchair. These stories are inspiring to all ages and illustrate that getting older doesn't mean that you have to stop being active in your community," adds Jillaina.

Wish of a Lifetime has granted more than 1,000 wishes to seniors in all 50 states. More significantly, over six years we've begun to spread the word about the importance of our senior population and how vital they have been, and still are, to our society.

Some Wishes Granted

In April 2014, *People* magazine ran a short story about a unique reunion of three sisters who had not seen each other in many years. Rose Shloss, a 101-year-old Wish of a Lifetime recipient, was reunited with her older sisters, Ruth Branum, 104, and Rubye Cox, 110. They are the remaining three of seven siblings, living in different parts of the country. The *People* magazine story, Facebook post, and video inspired nearly 100,000 "likes" and 20,000 shares. It was the kind of heartwarming story that brought attention to the foundation and inspiration to seniors everywhere.

Another wish: A former member of both the United States Navy and Air Force for ten years each, 84-year-old Dan wanted to return to an active submarine for a visit. He loved life in the submarines where he served as physician examiner and later as a surgeon in the Navy's submarine service.

During the Korean War, Dan traveled on multiple tours of sea duty aboard a submarine rescue vessel as well as in one of 12 submarines that were part of his squadron. The problem with getting Dr. Dan back on a submarine to fulfill his wish of a lifetime was the difficulty in climbing up and down the narrow ladders within the vessel. Dan had a short ladder built to practice climbing up and down until he felt he could handle the task. The staff at the King's Bay Naval Base in Georgia then supplied a special ladder/staircase on the USS Maryland, an active U.S. nuclear submarine, to make Dan's dream of being on a submarine again a reality.

Then there's 93-year-old Warren, of Troy, Ohio, who grew up working on a farm that had been in his family for more than 100 years. It was there that he had harvested corn, hay, and beans to make a living for his family. After Warren and his wife left the farm, they turned it over to their children. Warren wanted to see the farm from a new perspective—he wanted to look down at the land from a hot air balloon. Through the foundation, his wish came true and he got an aerial view of his family's legacy.

These are the kinds of wishes that come true and make everyone involved with Wish of a Lifetime beam with joy.

Your Own Legacy

"I think at the end of the day what will mark success for me will be what I've been able to do for other people," David Karnstedt says. "If the people you've worked with go off to higher levels of success, then you have had an impact. So I'd like my legacy to be about having influenced people positively in a way that they can go off and be successful at whatever it is they do."

DYING REGRETS

In 2013, *The Huffington Post* published the top five regrets of the dying, based on research on the topic.

1. I wish I'd had the courage to live a life true to myself, not the life others expected of me.

    "This was the most common regret of all. When people realize that their life is almost over and look back clearly on it, it is easy to see how many dreams have gone unfulfilled. Most people had not honored even a half of their dreams and had to die knowing that it was due to choices they had made, or not made. Health brings a freedom very few realize, until they no longer have it."

2. I wish I hadn't worked so hard.

    "This came from every male patient that I nursed. They missed their children's youth and their partner's companionship. Women also spoke of this regret, but as most were from an older generation, many of the female patients had not been breadwinners. All of the men I nursed deeply regretted spending so much of their lives on the treadmill of a work existence."

3. I wish I'd had the courage to express my feelings.

    "Many people suppressed their feelings in order to keep peace with others. As a result, they settled for a mediocre existence and never became who they were truly capable of becoming. Many developed illnesses relating to the bitterness and resentment they carried as a result."

4. I wish I had stayed in touch with my friends.

    "Often they would not truly realize the full benefits of old friends until their dying weeks and it was not always possible to track them down. Many had become so caught up in their own lives that they

DYING REGRETS, continued

had let golden friendships slip by over the years. There were many deep regrets about not giving friendships the time and effort that they deserved. Everyone misses their friends when they are dying."

5. I wish that I had let myself be happier.

"This is a surprisingly common one. Many did not realize until the end that happiness is a choice. They had stayed stuck in old patterns and habits. The so-called 'comfort' of familiarity overflowed into their emotions, as well as their physical lives. Fear of change had them pretending to others, and to their selves, that they were content, when deep within, they longed to laugh properly and have silliness in their life again."

Most often, I've found that legacies do not revolve around the letters people achieve after their names or how much money they made. When I looked at a study of people in hospice care, their greatest regrets were also not about money, but things like not letting themselves be happier more often, not spending enough time with friends, or not having the courage to express their feelings. These were personal thoughts and personal regrets.

Consider how Roger Staubach, who served in Vietnam and commanded 41 enlisted men, won two Super Bowl rings during an outstanding NFL career, and became an enormously successful real estate mogul, answered the question, "How do you want to be remembered?"

"I think the most important thing I'd like people to say about me is that he's been a faithful husband and good father," says Staubach. "I'm so proud to say I have five kids, 15 grandchildren, and one great-grandson. That's at the top of my list, and I feel very blessed. I'm always grateful that I got to play for a great football team and I had a great mentor in Mr. Miller in the real estate business. There are a lot of people

IT'S NOT ALWAYS GOOD TO BE KING: BUILDING A LEGACY

Sometimes an incredible legacy story comes late in life, as is the case for Brian Swette, who spent 17 years at PepsiCo and six years as the chairman of the board at Burger King.

"I tell people that the first 17 years my career was designed around getting people to drink larger and larger quantities of soda, and then I moved on to Burger King," says Swette, who considers his life after 60, as co-founder of Sweet Earth Natural Foods, to be a legacy project.

"My interest in sustainable healthy food came from the pivotal understanding that what I was doing wasn't good for anyone, as well as a maturity about how important a plant-based diet can be both for sustainability and health." Swette cites three factors that eventually changed the course of his life—the words of a departing staffer, his daughter, and a fortuitous invitation.

"At PepsiCo, a longtime employee walked up to me one day and told me he was quitting. It was right out of the blue, and I asked him why. He said three words: 'corn fructose syrup.' This was years ago, and I had no idea what he was talking about, so I asked him to be more specific. He said, 'It's a drug, it's evil, it's really bad, and it's hurting people,' so I started to investigate."

Swette also points to the time his daughter, while in high school and taking tests to get into a good college, told him that she had become a vegetarian. Concerned whether she would get enough protein, he once again investigated.

And finally, there was the Global Institute for Sustainability. "They had invited educators on sustainability along with people from the corporate

IT'S NOT ALWAYS GOOD TO BE KING: BUILDING A LEGACY, continued

world, which included me, coming from Burger King. I had little to say but learned a lot," explains Swette.

Roughly six years ago, Swette walked away from Burger King and the corporate world. Together with his wife, a former engineer at PepsiCo and ex-head of marketing at Calvin Klein, he started Sweet Earth Natural Foods. "It's all about meat-free, plant-based food that tastes good," says Swette, who says that he did everything that you are not supposed to do when starting a business, such as using your own money and entering the low-margin food business.

"I believe that this is a form of redemption," says Swette, adding, "I believe in second chances."

that have an effect on your life, and for that I'm thankful, but family is always most important to me."

I find it fascinating, the legacies that people build and how they want to be remembered. As hard as we strive for money, fame, and prestige in our careers, so many people look at those areas of life that touch other people. Helping other people and also learning from them puts so many aspects of life into proper perspective.

WHAT DOES IT ALL MEAN?

A s I said at the start of this book, I spent most of my life tirelessly chasing my biggest dreams in football and skiing. Along the way I accomplished most of my goals and fell short in a few.

I learned how champions persevere through adversity and use those lessons to refine their road map to success and established several principles that I believe are the keys to success.

First, I gave myself a set time in which to pick myself up after defeat or failure and move on, my 48-hour rule. Next, I decided not to read my own headlines or let my ego get in my way. If you have success, enjoy it, but do not let it become you—if you do, when you experience failure, that becomes who you are, too. I also made a very concerted effort to learn how to motivate myself intrinsically, based on doing the best that I could possibly do and not setting out to beat the competition or prove myself to other people. The transition from external motivation was not easy, but once I lost that need to please others, I felt better about myself and cleared my head to focus on my own abilities.

I planted many seeds so that I never had all my eggs in one basket. I found passions and investigated to see if they led to the right course for me. I've also tried to surround myself with positive, intelligent people who inspire and challenge me. Having people to talk to and learn from is so valuable. I've included the thoughts of some of my mentors in the pages of this book. They, and others, have provided me with knowledge and wisdom.

We can't accomplish every goal; however, the enriching experiences on the journey through life happen somewhere between the dream and reality, even if we fall a few times along the way. Impermanence is real; today is the youngest that you will ever be. I encourage you to dream. There are limitless opportunities for the unafraid.

I'll leave you with a quote that left an impression on me by Dylan Thomas:

"Do not go gentle into that good night,
Old age should burn and rave at close of day;
Rage, rage against the dying of the light."

ABOUT THE AUTHOR

Jeremy Bloom is CEO of the advertising technology company, Integrate, and founder of Wish of a Lifetime, a nonprofit organization. In addition to his professional life, Jeremy is an accomplished athlete in both skiing and football. He is a three-time World Champion, two-time Olympian, 11-time World Cup gold medalist and a member of the United States Skiing Hall of Fame. In 2005, he won a record six straight World Cup events, the most in a single season in the sport's history. He was also an All-American football player at the University of Colorado and played professional football as a wide receiver and return specialist in the National Football League for the Philadelphia Eagles and the Pittsburgh Steelers.

While playing with the NFL in Philadelphia for the Eagles, he completed a business entrepreneurship program at Wharton Business School where he studied real estate and finance. In addition to his athletic achievements, Jeremy possesses a driving motivation to give back to those around him. His desire to impact the lives of others led to The Wish of a Lifetime Foundation, which grants lifelong wishes to people ages 70, 80, 90, and even 100. The nonprofit has granted over 1,000 wishes across the United States and throughout Canada. In 2009, Jeremy entered the business world where he ran marketing efforts for MDinfo.com, a health portal creating a dialogue between health experts and individuals throughout the world. In April 2010, Jeremy cofounded the marketing software company Integrate, the first advertising technology provider that automates customer generation for B2B marketers. Through Jeremy's vision and leadership Integrate was named as the "Best New Company" at the 2011 American Business Awards in New York City. Also in 2011 Jeremy was named by Forbes as one of the 30 under 30, featuring executives under the age of 30 making waves in the technology realm. In 2013, Jeremy was a finalist for the Ernst & Young Entrepreneur of the Year.

Outside of business, Jeremy has continued to maintain his name within the sports world. He does commentary for college football and is an Olympic Sports Television Analyst. He has worked for ESPN, Fox, NBC, and The Pac-12 Network.

INDEX

A

accepting and moving on, 13–17, 28, 30–34, 133

admitting failure, 32–34. *See also* embracing failure

adversity, 14, 16, 18, 86–87

Apple Inc., 21, 60

Avon, 61

B

Barnett, Gary, 7, 22

Bates, Tony, 49, 73, 94–95, 110, 112

Besner, Greg, 92–93, 95, 104–105

Bock, Laszlo, 81–84, 104

bottom-up management, 80, 81

bouncers, 14

Branson, Richard, 22

Brin, Sergey, 64, 96

Buckner, Bill, 22

business opportunities, 54, 56–60

C

career transitioning, 71

Carroll, Andy, 6

change, being open to, 60–63

co-founders, 82–84

Cogan, Karen, 27, 28

Comic-Con, 32

communication, 99–101, 102

competency, 106

compromise, 84

confidentiality, 97

conflict resolution, 83–84

corporate culture, 91–106. *See also* team building

building a strong culture, 64, 92

characteristics of strong, 93

cornerstones of, 95–101

cultural fit, 84, 104–106

cultural risk and, 95

demotivating employees and, 103

employee engagement and, 92

employee stake in, 106

hiring and, 104–106

management style and, 80–81

monitoring and evaluating, 105–106

optimism delusion and, 102

organizational design and, 101–102

secretiveness in, 91

transparency in, 81, 91–92, 94, 96, 97. *See also* secretive organizations

workplace motivators and, 44–46, 103

Cultural Cycle, The (Heskett), 93

cultural fit, 84, 104–106. *See also* corporate culture

curveballs, 58

customers, communicating with, 99–101

D

Datalogix, 61–63

Davis, Tony, 5

deadline for accepting failure, 13–17, 133

definitions of failure, 26–27

demotivating employees, 103

Difference Maker, The (Maxwell), 14

distractions, 2, 18–19, 23–24, 111–113. *See also* focus

Dowling, John, 5

E

Eagles, 10, 79, 80–81

ego reprogramming, 38–46

ego-driven behavior, 36–38, 85–86, 133

Elway, John, 4–5, 20

embracing failure, 28, 30–34

emergent leaders, 104

emotional neutrality, 20, 113–114

employees

communicating with, 99, 101, 102

corporate culture and. *See* corporate culture

demotivating, 103

empowering, 97

hiring, 104–106

physical space for, 99

time off for, 96–97, 98

workplace motivators and, 44–46, 103

empowering employees, 97

endorphins, 113

Enemies of Exploration: Self-initiated vs. Other-initiated Learning (Condry), 44

entrepreneurship, 64

even-keeled emotions, 20, 113–114

examining failures, 14–15, 27–28

exercise, 113

extrinsic motivation, 36, 41

F

FailCon, 32

failure, definitions of, 26–27

failure leading to failure, 28

fear of embracing failure, 28, 32–33

Feld, Brad, 40, 96

Finkelstein, Sydney, 27–28

Flickr, 60

focus, 2, 17–20, 23–24, 29, 51, 111–113

forty-eight hour rule, 13–17, 133

G

giving up, 29, 32

goals

developing options, 4–11, 22–24, 48, 52–53, 134

focusing on, 23–24
loftiness of, 28–30
refocusing, 29
reviewing and evaluating, 50
setting, 22–24, 48–49, 56
Gordon, Bing, 40
Groupon, 60

H
Harding, Tanya, 37
Hastings, Reed, 93
humility, 33, 86, 104
Hurley, Chad, 64, 104

I
inspiration, 41
Integrate, 48
intention, 49
intrinsic motivation, 36, 38–46, 134
investing in businesses, 54

J
Jobs, Steve, 21–22, 68

K
Karnstedt, David, 73, 100, 127
Keller, Katherine, 56
Kerrigan, Nancy, 37
Key Performance Indicators (KPI), 98–99
Kodak, 38, 51
Kries, Doc, 6

L
leaders, 84, 86–87, 89, 104
learning from failure, 14–15, 59
legacy building, 118–120, 127–131
Lego, 60
life-work balance, 96–97
Lightner, Candy, 89
LinkedIn, 72
Linnemen, Peter, 54
living downstairs, 2, 18–19. *See also* focus

loftiness of goals, 28–30

M
management styles, 80–81
managing risk, 111. *See also* risk
Marchetti, Chris, 7
Maris, Bill, 64, 104
MDinfo Inc., 56–60
mental keys, 17–20
milestones, 51–52
mind like a river, 2, 17–18. *See also* focus
Minshew, Kathryn, 30
Mothers Against Drunk Driving (MADD), 89
motivation
bottom-up management and, 80, 81
ego-driven, 36–38, 85–86, 133
extrinsic, 36, 41
failure as source of, 33
intrinsic, 36, 38–46, 134
top-down management and, 80–81
workplace motivators, 44–46, 103
moving on, 13–17, 28, 30–34, 133
Mycoskie, Blake, 45

N
Nadal, Rafael, 40–41
negative embracement of failure, 32
negative thoughts, 2, 17–18. *See also* focus
NeST Software Inc., 21
networking, 72
NeXT Computer Inc., 21
NextAction, 61–63
NFL Combine (2006), 4–5, 10, 15–16
noise/distractions, 2, 18–19, 23–24, 111–113. *See also* focus

Nokia, 60
nonprofits, 122–127

O

Objectives and Key Results (OKR)
management system, 98–99
Ohno, Apolo, 68–71, 114–115
Olympics in Salt Lake City (Winter
2002), 9–10
Olympics in Torino (Winter 2006),
1, 2–4, 9–10
optimism delusion, 102
organizational design, 101–102

P

partnerships, 82–84
passion, 21–22, 48–49, 53–60,
73–74, 134
perception of failure, 31
personal road map. *See* road map
for success
personal satisfaction, 36, 38–46,
134
Philadelphia Eagles, 10, 79, 80–81
physical space, 99
Pittsburgh Steelers, 81
pivoting, 60–63
Pixar Animation Studios, 21
planning for success, 49–53
planting seeds, 22–24, 48, 52–53,
134
positive embracement of failure,
33–34
Power of Intention, The (Dyer), 36–37,
40
pressures, 18–19
PYP Media, 30

R

Rawles, Scott, 5, 6
recovering from failure, 30–31
redefining yourself, 67–77

reference checking, 86
regrets of the dying, 128–129
Reid, Andy, 10, 80, 81
resiliency, 21–22
respect, 104
Riley, Pat, 37
risk, 28–30, 33, 107–111, 114–115
road map for success, 47–65
guidelines for, 64–65
milestone setting for, 51–52
passion and, 53–60
pivoting and, 60–63
planning, 49–53
planting seeds for, 52–53
Roza, Eric, 33, 61–63, 96

S

Sagel, Gail, 69–70
Schell, Cooper, 19
Schwartz, Tony, 98
secretive organizations, 91. *See also*
transparency
seed planting, 22–24, 48, 52–53,
134
self-defeating thoughts, 2, 17–18.
See also focus
self-esteem, 38
self-satisfaction, 36, 38–46, 134
skills, focusing on, 2, 19–20
splatters, 14
Staubach, Roger, 74–76, 129
Steelers, 81
stress, 113
success, 36, 41, 58. *See also* road
map for success
Swette, Brian, 130–131

T

team building, 79–90. *See also*
corporate culture
building strong teams, 81–86

intrinsic motivation and, 46
leaders vs. victims, 86–90
management style in, 80–81
optimism delusion and, 102
tenacity, 21
TGIF calls, 96
time off, 96–97, 98
Tomizuka, David, 33, 97–98
Tomlin, Mike, 10, 81, 114
TOMS, 45
top-down management, 80–81
transparency, 81, 91–92, 94, 96, 97.
  See also secretive organizations
tunnel vision, 2, 18–19. *See also*
  focus

V

Vaughan, Scott, 97–98
victims, 87–90

W

Wachendorf, Jillaina, 126
Wallace, Christina, 30–31
ways to fail, 27–28
weight of failure, 28–30, 31, 59
Why Smart Executives Fail
  (Finkelstein), 27
Wilson, Chris, 55
winning, 35–44
Wish of a Lifetime (WOL), 23,
  122–127
work-life integration, 96–97
workplace motivators, 44–46, 103
World Cup skiing, 2, 6–8, 17–18,
  36, 39–40
Wozniak, Steve, 21